RECLAIMING LOV

"I owe so much to Ajith Fernando. ⬚⬚⬚⬚⬚⬚⬚⬚⬚⬚⬚,
he lives it. His authenticity and sel⬚⬚⬚⬚⬚⬚⬚⬚⬚⬚⬚t
conditions challenge me deeply."

—Tim Stafford, award-winning author,
and senior writer for *Christianity Today*

"Christians today often are quick to argue for truth, but we are sometimes slow to live by the fundamental virtue of love. I know Ajith Fernando as a man of God who lives what he preaches. His focus in this book is one desperately needed in the church today: love, sacrifice, and forgiveness. Such a lifestyle flows most readily from a genuine trust in God, who vindicates those who serve others unselfishly."

—Craig Keener, Professor of New Testament,
Asbury Theological Seminary

"Soul-searching insights to the practical outworking of 1 Corinthians 13. Giving the book a ring of authenticity, Ajith writes of his own ministry of compassion across the years. As few persons I know, his lifestyle models what he teaches. For persons wanting help in expressing love to hurting, broken people, this book could hardly be better."

—Robert E. Coleman, Distinguished Senior Professor of Evangelism and Discipleship at Gordon-Conwell Theological Seminary

"Love as the ultimate Christian distinctive derives from the New Testament's unique concept and proof of God's unconditional love in the Lord Jesus. Ajith Fernando's practical exposition of the eternal superlative reflects the simplicity, authenticity, and risk of loving in difficult contexts of human odium. *Reclaiming Love* again reveals Ajith's personable freshness: explanation generated from Bible study, illustration from deep and wide experience, and application grown out of his own bold obedience. Most can write on love. Ajith lives love. Here's a thought-evoking, heart-provoking work for your knowing, being, doing, and especially loving."

—Ramesh Richard, Dallas Theological Seminary

"Ajith Fernando has been ministering in the name of the Lord Jesus Christ for over three decades on several continents. Out of his love for the Lord and hurting people, this anointed pastor, teacher, evangelist, and New Testament scholar has written a brilliantly refreshing book on 1 Corinthians 13. *Reclaiming Love* is rich in sound biblical exegesis and illustrations from real life. Anyone who reads this engagingly written book will be inspired, instructed, and better equipped to enter the cosmic battle for souls. I recommend it with enthusiasm."

—Lyle W. Dorsett, Beeson Divinity School

"What becomes immediately obvious in reading *Reclaiming Love* is that the author's heart has been plowed by the truths of this great love passage—for over forty years. That is why it is so penetrating. Indeed, the layered applications are sweetly surgical. Readers will incur deep bleeding furrows in their own souls, which will then invite the healing touch of the Master's hand."

—R. Kent Hughes, Senior Pastor Emeritus,
College Church in Wheaton

"In *Reclaiming Love*, Ajith Fernando reminds Christian leaders what matters most. Combining his profound grasp of Scripture and years of faithful service in ministry, he richly unfolds and perceptively applies 1 Corinthians 13, the Bible's great love chapter, for the complexities of our times. Read it and be challenged, instructed, inspired, and empowered to love."

—Stephen A. Seamands, Asbury Theological Seminary

RECLAIMING
LOVE

FOREWORD BY
RAVI ZACHARIAS

RECLAIMING
LOVE

RADICAL RELATIONSHIPS
IN A COMPLEX WORLD

AJITH
FERNANDO

ZONDERVAN

Reclaiming Love
Copyright © 2013 by Ajith Fernando

This title is also available as a Zondervan ebook.

Requests for information should be addressed to:
Zondervan, 3900 Sparks Dr. SE, Grand Rapids, Michigan 49546

This edition: ISBN 978-0-310-52336-9 (softcover)

Library of Congress Cataloging-in-Publication Data

Fernando, Ajith.
    Reclaiming love: radical relationships in a complex world / Ajith Fernando.
    p. cm.
    Includes bibliographical references
    ISBN 978-0-310-49278-8
    1. Love—Religious aspects—Christianity. 2. Interpersonal relations—Religious
aspects—Christianity. I. Title.
BV4639.F397 2013
241'.4—dc23
2012039884

Scripture quotations marked ESV are taken from the ESV® Bible (The Holy Bible, English Standard Version®). Copyright © 2001 by Crossway, a publishing ministry of Good News Publishers. Used by permission. All rights reserved.

Any Internet addresses (websites, blogs, etc.) and telephone numbers in this book are offered as a resource. They are not intended in any way to be or imply an endorsement by Zondervan, nor does Zondervan vouch for the content of these sites and numbers for the life of this book.

All royalties from the sale of this book have been assigned to literature and education projects through Youth for Christ, Sri Lanka: 25 Kassapa Road, Columbo 5 00500, Sri Lanka.

Cover design: Micah Kandros Design
Cover photography or illustration: Veer
Interior design: Matthew Van Zomeren

Printed in the United States of America

To
Rabindranath Refuge
and
Cheryl Fernando.
We thank God for his wonderful answer
to over two decades of earnest prayer
that God would give godly spouses to our children.

CONTENTS

BIBLE TRANSLATIONS USED

FOREWORD
RAVI ZACHARIAS, AUTHOR AND SPEAKER

IN HIS GREAT CHAPTER 13 in 1 Corinthians, the apostle Paul concludes, "And now these three remain: faith, hope and love. But the greatest of these is love" (verse 13). These are the elements of life without which it is impossible to live. *Faith* is that aspect built on a relationship between the truth we know and the truth we have yet to learn, as we enlarge our knowledge into the unknown. *Hope* casts a long shadow, even in times when it seems to have disappeared. But then comes the greatest—*love*. It is the supreme value and the supreme expression in a world where so often hate seems to have won the day.

As humans we long for love that brings hope and restores broken relationships. Indeed, God's vision for humanity is that we might see his claim on us as an invitation to live and love. God offered up his own Son to pain and death because of his marvelous, unfathomable love for the world. This is the amazing story of the gospel.

It is obvious that the greatest of loves comes at the greatest cost. Such love will never come cheaply. Sometimes it takes everything you have to honor love, and it takes everything you have to honor trust. What I heard from a doctor from another faith whom I met in Pakistan and who had come to know Christ comes to my mind often. He told me about the two sentences spoken from a preacher that changed his life: "In surrendering, you win. In dying, you live."

We are meant to be the hands and the arms of God. The church is called not only to bring people to God but also to take God to those who are wounded by the experiences of trying to live in this world, to touch those who are broken, to bring healing to those with damaged emotions. Meeting people where they are hurting is a vital aspect of our call to reflect God to the society in which we live.

I have known Ajith Fernando for more than three decades, and he has a unique capacity to meet people where they are hurting, whether speaking to an audience of one or one thousand. Together we have followed our separate callings to preach the gospel—the good news that God has provided a way for our redemption and our forgiveness to bring us back into relationship with him. The gospel is beautiful. It is true. It brings hope. It has transforming power.

Ajith Fernando is one of the finest biblical expositors of our time and a keenly insightful cross-cultural communicator. But he is more. He is also a friend to youth, the poor, and the downtrodden, and God has used Ajith's preaching, perceptiveness, and pathos to transform countless lives.

Reclaiming Love reflects a lifetime of wisdom from a seasoned counselor, leader, and Bible scholar. It is a masterful study of a familiar yet difficult-to-apply chapter on love. We long for a corrective within. We long for beautiful relationships. As Ajith illustrates, those two realities are made possible only through Jesus Christ, who enables us to persevere, to forgive, to surrender, and to hope. That is love and that is the gospel. I have learned much from Ajith over the years, and I know that you will be enriched as you study this book and consider the great truths of 1 Corinthians 13. I wholeheartedly recommend *Reclaiming Love*.

PREFACE

DURING THREE AND A HALF DECADES of ministry in Youth for Christ and in the church to which we belong, God seems to have chosen to send our way many people who are bruised and battered from the dysfunctional environments in which they grew up. Helping nurture them to follow the Christian ethic of love has been a great challenge, and I have seen much failure along the way. But I have also seen some who have been transformed to become Christlike people. Moreover, we have had to live with the ravages of the civil war that engulfed our country for thirty years. So I have been grappling with the question of how we can apply the biblical teachings about love in such situations for many years.

Working with extreme situations has, I believe, yielded insights that will help all Christians—even those who haven't gone through the extremely painful experiences of the people I have encountered. This is what made me decide to share the results of my grappling with a wider audience.

The one fundamental of the Christian faith with which I have struggled most is that it is possible to practice what the Word of God teaches about love and holiness. Applying this truth in my personal life and in the lives of those among whom I have ministered has been, to put it mildly, a challenge. Whenever I preach on 1 Corinthians 13, I've had to preach first to myself.

Many of those to whom we have ministered, coming from tough backgrounds, have ended up on the staff of Youth for Christ. Trying to disciple and pastor them has been my major ministry challenge during the past few years. We have been happy to see a somewhat better rate of success with our staff.

I started teaching on 1 Corinthians 13 about thirty years ago. I first began to teach it to our staff and volunteers and then to a wider spectrum of audiences both in Sri Lanka and abroad. I realized that I must put the material I was teaching into writing. I am grateful for a month I spent at

Hollywood Presbyterian Church in 2001, where I was able to hide and write another book while preaching on 1 Corinthians 13. This gave me the opportunity to start preparing a series on love afresh.

I am happy to be working with Zondervan again and benefitting from their professional expertise.

I want to express my gratitude for some of the greatest human beings through whom God's love was modeled and mediated to my life. I thank God for the family in which I grew up. Whenever I think of my parents and siblings, it has always been with joyous gratitude. I also thank God for my pastor during my teenage years, Irish missionary the late Rev. George Good, whose life exemplified the beauty of Christian love. He preached a wonderful series on 1 Corinthians 13 at a pastors' conference during the early years of my ministry that alerted me to the potency of this passage.

I have often felt joyfully unworthy of receiving so much love and security from [my wife, Nelun,] our children, Nirmali and Asiri, and the family of Youth for Christ, of which I have been privileged to be a member for forty-six years. Nelun and I feel that with this privilege comes the responsibility and call to minister God's love to bruised and broken people. In this process it has been a joy to observe how Nelun lives 1 Corinthians 13 in practice better than I ever could. I have dedicated this book to our two children-in-law, whom we have joyfully grafted into our family and whose love we have received with much joy and gratitude.

Finally, how could I ever write on love without acknowledging the astounding display of love by God in providing for us a way of salvation, in displaying his amazing love in the life of Jesus, and in pouring out his love into our hearts through the Holy Spirit? His love is what empowers us and helps us to express radical love in a complex world.

Note: I have made slight changes in the details of some of the stories in this book so that what actually happened would be communicated without the risk of the persons described in the story being identified.

1 CORINTHIANS 12:31–13:13
ENGLISH STANDARD VERSION

12:31But earnestly desire the higher gifts. And I will show you a still more excellent way.

13:1If I speak in the tongues of men and of angels, but have not love, I am a noisy gong or a clanging cymbal. 2And if I have prophetic powers, and understand all mysteries and all knowledge, and if I have all faith, so as to remove mountains, but have not love, I am nothing. 3If I give away all I have, and if I deliver up my body to be burned, but have not love, I gain nothing.

4Love is patient and kind; love does not envy or boast; it is not arrogant 5or rude. It does not insist on its own way; it is not irritable or resentful; 6it does not rejoice at wrongdoing, but rejoices with the truth. 7Love bears all things, believes all things, hopes all things, endures all things.

8Love never ends. As for prophecies, they will pass away; as for tongues, they will cease; as for knowledge, it will pass away. 9For we know in part and we prophesy in part, 10but when the perfect comes, the partial will pass away. 11When I was a child, I spoke like a child, I thought like a child, I reasoned like a child. When I became a man, I gave up childish ways. 12For now we see in a mirror dimly, but then face to face. Now I know in part; then I shall know fully, even as I have been fully known.

13So now faith, hope, and love abide, these three; but the greatest of these is love.

FOLLOWING THE WAY OF LOVE

1 CORINTHIANS 12:31

IF YOU HAVE EVER BEEN in the midst of a deeply focused conversation on a particular topic, only to have it abruptly ended when someone brings up something new for discussion, you know how frustrating it feels to be interrupted. At other times, however, we are more than happy to be interrupted. When someone interrupts our work to share good news, announcing an engagement or the birth of a baby, we are excited to hear what they have to share. In my homeland of Sri Lanka, for example, no one minds in the least if you break into a conversation with a cricket score (though that might not be true elsewhere in the world). First Corinthians 13 falls into that category of interruption.

First Corinthians 12 and 14 address issues that had arisen in the church of Corinth about the use of the gifts of the Spirit. There is an abrupt change in the middle of that discussion with the insertion of the famous love chapter. The Corinthian Christians seem to have placed so much value in exercising gifts that displayed the power of God in their life that they did so selfishly and failed to display the character of God. Paul wants these Christians to get their priorities straight. First they needed to be godly people. Only then they could be agents of his power.

GOD PROVIDES THE LOVE—WE OBEY

Paul founded the church in Corinth around the midpoint of the first century, during his second missionary journey. A few years later he received some disturbing reports about doctrinal confusion and disturbing practices and sins in that church (1 Cor. 5:1; 11:18). The Corinthian Christians also wrote him a letter seeking clarification on certain doctrinal and practical matters (cf. 7:1). The first letter to the Corinthians is Paul's response to these reports and to the letter the church in Corinth had sent. Among the issues in their letter were questions about the use of the gifts of the Spirit in the church (12:1). This issue seems to have triggered some conflicts in the church. Paul's answer to these questions covers 1 Corinthians 12 to 14. Chapters 12 and 14 deal with practical issues regarding the use of gifts. In chapter 13 Paul inserts into his exposition something far more important than gifts that the Corinthians should be focusing their attention on: love.

Believers in the church at Corinth seem to have had a hierarchy of gifts, depending on the usefulness of each gift to the church. Paul's major theme in chapter 14 is that while tongues builds up the individual believer, prophecy builds up the church. Therefore for use in the church, prophesy is a more useful gift to exercise when the church meets. That debate seems to serve as the background of the statement in 12:31: "But earnestly desire the higher gifts" (1Cor. 12:31a). Since some gifts are more helpful to the body, desire those gifts, says Paul.

Earlier he had referred to the "Spirit, who apportions to each one individually as he wills" (1 Cor. 12:11). We can desire the more helpful gifts, but it is God who decides who gets which gift. While we can ask God for a certain gift, we have no guarantee that we will receive that gift. Now he presents something about which there is no such uncertainty. He says, "And I will show you a still more excellent way" (12:31). This is not an optional desire; this is the "way" Christians live. Chapter 13 shows us that he is talking about love. In 14:1 he forcefully presents the implications of the fact that love is a way to follow by saying, "Pursue" or "Follow the way of love" (NIV). An older translation renders this, "Make love your aim" (RSV). Now our ambition in life is to love.

We cannot say, "God did not give me the ability to love." In every situation, whether we like it or not, we follow the way of love. When our neighbor is sick in the hospital, we cannot say, "But I do not like going to the hospital." When a little boy calls his father to play a game with him, he cannot say, "But I prefer to watch television at this time." When a woman is faced with the need to forgive the man who insulted her husband, she cannot say, "That is too hurtful a thing for me to forgive." Later in this book we will look at some of the processes that go on in the mind before we are ready to forgive. But the command to love our enemy remains unchanged.

When our commander says, "Forward march," we cannot say, "Let me first have a cup of tea." Love is the way we follow; it is not an option.

So for the Christian, love is a priority; it is an act of obedience. Looking at the way Christian love is described in the Bible, we realize that it is not a case of loving the lovable. Rather, it includes loving our enemies, blessing those who persecute us, being patient with people who are difficult to tolerate, visiting prisoners, and the like. These are actions that do not automatically happen, like falling in love. Christian love is decisive; we must make it happen.

That is one side of the story. The other side is that the love with which we love is God's love in us. John said, "We love because he first loved us" (1 John 4:19). Paul explains that this is done by the Holy Spirit. Love is the first aspect of the fruit of the Spirit (Gal. 5:22). The apostle says in Romans 5:5: "God's love has been poured into our hearts through the Holy Spirit who has been given to us" (Rom. 5:5). The word translated "poured" has the idea of abundance. J. B. Phillips renders it as "flooding."[1] The great British commentator C. E. B. Cranfield writes that this word "may well have been chosen in order to express the idea of unstinting lavishness."[2] God's love is an inexhaustible resource coming from his eternal reservoir. And that is not all. This "love of Christ compels us" (2 Cor. 5:14a NIV). The word translated "compels" has the idea of applying pressure.

The idea we get from these verses is that God's love enters us and then pushes us to act in love. Our part is to obey. Obedience is the key that opens the floodgates of God's love, so that we will be supplied with the strength to love in the way the Bible asks us to. So while the Holy Spirit gives us love as his fruit (Gal. 5:22), our job is to "keep step with the Spirit" (Gal. 5:25 NIV), through obedience. If we do not love when we should, we "quench" (or "stifle," NLT) the Holy Spirit (1 Thess. 5:19).

Corrie ten Boom was imprisoned along with her two sisters, Betsie and Nollie, her brother Willem, and her father for having hidden Jews in their home during the Second World War. Her father died ten days after their arrest, and Nollie and Willem were released from prison shortly after their arrest. Betsie died much later after she and Corrie had spent some time in a concentration camp. Corrie was finally released because of a clerical error. Two years after the war ended, Corrie had just finished speaking at a meeting in Munich when she saw one of the terrible guards from her concentration camp standing in a line to meet her. Immediately, her mind flashed back to an image of her sister Betsie walking past this man, stripped of all her clothes and dignity. Now, that same guard was standing in front of Corrie with his hand thrust out.

"A fine message, *Fräulein!*" he said. "How good it is to know that, as you say, all our sins are at the bottom of the sea."

Corrie had just spoken on the topic of forgiveness. But rather than taking the man's hand, she fumbled with her pocketbook. The guard informed her that he had been a guard at Ravensbrück and added, "But since that time I have become a Christian. I know that God has forgiven me for the cruel things I did there. But I would like to hear it from your lips as well."

Again, his hand came out, "*Fräulein,* will you forgive me?"

Corrie writes, "I stood there — I whose sins had every day to be forgiven — and I could not. Betsie had died in that place. Could he erase her slow terrible death simply for the asking?"

As Corrie stood there, she pondered a difficult choice. She knew, in her heart, that there was no question of *not* forgiving, for she understood that "the message that God forgives has a prior condition: that we forgive those who have injured us." In fact, she had just spoken of the necessity of forgiveness, of the need to forgive as God has forgiven us in Christ. Corrie also knew that, after the war, "those who were able to forgive their former enemies were able also to return to the outside world and rebuild their lives, no matter what the physical scars. Those who nursed bitterness remained invalids."

"And still," says Corrie, "I stood there with the coldness clutching my heart." Emotionally frozen, Corrie reasoned that "forgiveness is not an emotion." Instead, she reminded herself that forgiveness "is an act of the will, and the will can function regardless of the temperature of the heart." She silently prayed, "Jesus help me! I can lift my hand. I can do that much. You supply the feeling.... And so woodenly, mechanically, I stretched my hand to the one stretched out to me."

Just at that time something amazing happened. "The current started in my shoulder, raced down my arm, sprang into our joined hands. And then this healing warmth seemed to flood my whole being, bringing tears to my eyes."

Corrie cried out, "I forgive you, brother! With all my heart!"

Corrie then writes about the incident: "For a long moment we grasped each other's hands, the former guard and the former prisoner. I have never known God's love so intensely as I did then."[3]

We wrongly assume that we must feel something before we can do it.

We conclude that loving emotions must always precede loving actions. But psychologists tell us that while it is true that our *emotions* affect our actions, it is equally true that our *actions* affect our emotions. "We are not to sit and wait for loving feelings to come for some brother or sister; we are to do some loving action for them and the feelings will follow."[4] So Christian love is decisive love. And that often means loving when you don't feel like doing so.

Can you see the three steps in the process of God's love being activated and used in Corrie's life? First, God's love applied pressure on Corrie to forgive. Second, Corrie decided to obey God's command, even though she did not feel like doing so. Third, God supplied the strength to follow through with the decision to lovingly obey.

I counted fifty-one commands to love in the New Testament. I think the Bible commands us to love so often because loving is often contrary to our natural inclination. When someone has hurt us, we simply do not feel like responding to that person in love. If you are angry about being unfairly overlooked for a certain responsibility, you do not feel like responding positively when the leader asks you again because the person who was first offered the responsibility refused it. You want to express your displeasure by refusing to take the job on. But despite your natural inclination, you know you must take it on because the Bible commands you to love in such situations. I can assure you that you will not regret it. God will honor your decision to love by providing you the divine strength you need to do the job.

AGAPĒ: THE FAVORITE CHRISTIAN WORD FOR LOVE

There are different Greek words for love in the New Testament, but we should be careful about making too much of the differences between those words. Words take on meanings according to the context in which they appear. The commonest words for love in the New Testament are the noun *agapē* (116 times) and the verb *agapaō* (143 times). While the verb *agapaō* was common in the Greek translation of the Old Testament (the Septuagint), the noun *agapē* appeared there only 20 times. In the literature outside the New Testament the noun *philia* was more common than *agapē*, but it appears only once in the New Testament. The corresponding verb *phileō* appears 25 times in the New Testament. Without making too much of distinction between these and other words for love, we cannot help noticing the unusual popularity of the relatively uncommon words *agapē* and *agapaō* rather than the more common words *philia* and *phileō*.

Many scholars think that the reason for the popularity of *agapē* in the New Testament was the desire of the early Christians to affirm that Christian love was unique. The commoner words would possibly be associated with sub-Christian understandings of love. This may be the reason why the Italian scholar Jerome (who lived from around AD 345 to around AD 419) used the word [*caritas*] rather than the more common *amor* to designate Christian love in his influential translation of the Bible into Latin called the Vulgate.[5] That seems to have been closer to the idea of Christian love being a decisive action. This undoubtedly influenced the translators of the King James Version to use often the English word "charity" for Christian love in the Bible.

LOVE IS AN END IN ITSELF

Implied in Paul's description of love as the "more excellent way" (12:31) is the idea that love is more than a means to an end; it is an end in itself. This is more explicit in the admonition to "pursue love" (14:1), or as the RSV renders it, "make love your aim." Elsewhere Paul says, "The aim of our charge is love" (1 Tim. 1:5). Love is one of our key goals in life even though it is difficult to measure.

Measurable goals are important. In today's rushed and competitive world, it is not enough to say, "I worked hard." If we work hard without any goals and with no results to show, we can easily get left behind, especially in our workplace. We must find the best way to achieve the most in the shortest possible time and with the use of the least resources. So we are always looking for new and effective methods. These things are necessary for progress and productivity in today's world.

But this is not all that there is to life. There is a deeper and more basic aspect of life that determines our highest ambitions. Being made in the image of the God who is love (1 John 4:8), humans achieve their full humanity only when they live lives of love. Sometimes we love people with a measurable goal in view. So love makes us help a student with her studies so that she will do well at her exams. Love makes us train a young athlete so that he will win a gold medal at an athletic meet. These are good examples of love expressed with specific goals in mind.

Sometimes, however, we love people even though there does not seem to be a measurable goal that is achievable through our acts of love. Mother

Theresa's Sisters of Charity achieved fame and esteem by caring for help-less dying paupers, washing their soiled clothes and helping them die with dignity. Some parents wonder whether their decision to adopt a child was the right decision because the child rebelled and brought much pain to the parents. That does not negate the value of what they did for this child. He was given a chance to thrive in life. The fact that he did not turn out the way they hoped does not negate the value of what they did. This child may turn to God so that these anguished parents' prayers are answered, perhaps after they die. But even if he does not, what they did was good and fruitful.

A few minutes before writing these words, I was mourning the fact that I had helped someone at considerable cost and he had not turned out the way I hoped. The thought came to me that I had wasted my time and energy and suffered unnecessarily. Writing the earlier paragraph minis-tered to me! When we love, we are achieving the basic goal in the life of a Christian. Love is not only a means to an end; it is an end in itself.

In the late 1980s, I grew to appreciate the writings of Robertson McQuilkin, president of Columbia International University. In 1990, I was surprised to learn that McQuilkin had decided to resign from his position at the school. At the time, McQuilkin was in his prime, enjoy-ing worldwide influence as an internationally respected Christian leader. I later learned that McQuilkin had resigned in order to care full-time for his wife, who was suffering from Alzheimer's disease. After grappling for some time with a need to care for his wife in her deteriorating condition, he had finally decided that his primary responsibility at that stage of his life was caring for her, the woman who had stood by him and cared for him for over four decades.

His decision was not an easy one. Just three years after his decision to resign from Columbia, McQuilkin's wife could no longer even recognize him. It would have been tempting, at this point, to hire someone else to care for her and return to his work as a Christian leader. Yet until her death in 2003, for over ten years, McQuilkin chose to continue to serve his wife, providing her with the daily care she needed. Some might have considered this act of loving service a waste of his gifts. After all, McQuilkin could have hired a nurse or paid someone else to do this work. But Robertson McQuilkin understood that love is not the means to a greater end—it *is* itself the end to which God calls us.

Upon announcing his resignation from his position as the president of the university, McQuilkin spoke about the reason why he was leaving. He spoke of his deep and abiding love for his wife and concluded by adding, "She is such a delight to me, I don't *have* to care for her. I *get* to."[6]

So just the act of loving is an achievement. We live in a world where people have been discarded by others who should have been committed to them. The idea of long-term commitment is a culturally alien concept to people. People leave jobs, groups, friends, spouses, and parents when it is inconvenient and a hindrance to their progress in life. And what is the result? It is an insecure generation that lacks the joy of having people who are truly committed to them. In this environment, how health-giving is the experience of being loved at great cost by people who are doing so not with an ulterior motive but with an attitude that looks at loving as an achievement! Using the language of competition, Paul says, "Outdo one another in showing honor" (Rom. 12:10). The achievement here is honoring someone else, not gaining some earthly success for ourselves.

Christians who approach life in this way will be happy people. Other people may not respond to their actions in the way they hoped. But this does not leave believers disillusioned and angry—a condition that describes many people involved in humanitarian service. When we have loved, we have been successful. God has seen and he will reward. So our actions have not been meaningless or foolish.

CHAPTER 1

GREATER THAN SPECTACULAR GIFTS

1 CORINTHIANS 13:1-2

WHEN I WAS A CHILD, I imagined myself performing amazing feats of strength. I pictured myself jumping off a high balcony and rescuing a young girl, all without getting hurt or breaking into a sweat. I imagined that everyone would be mesmerized by my displays of heroism and power. Like any child, I wondered what it would be like to have super powers of flight and strength that would make people take notice of me.

In the church today we find many Christians who desire what are commonly known as "the sign gifts" — things like speaking in tongues, prophecy, and exercising miraculous powers. These gifts are the "super powers" of the New Testament. Not only are they exciting to use; they make everyone else sit up and take notice. So it's interesting to find that in the first two verses of 1 Corinthians 13, Paul gives us a sobering corrective to an overemphasis on these spectacular gifts. In essence, Paul tells us that such gifts are useless if love is absent from our lives.

Paul presents the challenging words of verses 1–3 in the first person ("I"). He does this elsewhere in his other letters when he talks about our battle for personal holiness (e.g., Rom. 7:7–25; Phil. 3:8–14). So why does he use the first person here in 1 Corinthians 13:1–3? While we cannot know all of his reasons, I think at least one is clear: Paul understands that those who preach to others must *first* learn to preach to themselves.

Though I have often preached on this chapter, I find I am still challenged each and every time I speak and teach on it. It's a wonderful reminder that we should bring to our reading of God's Word a sober openness to being disturbed by God's Spirit. Whether for personal study or for preparation for a ministry opportunity, we should always approach the Scriptures with the attitude of David when he prayed: "Search me, O God, and know my heart! Try me and know my thoughts! And see if there be any grievous way in me, and lead me in the way everlasting!" (Ps. 139:23–24).

TONGUES OF MEN AND ANGELS

Paul begins this chapter with these words: "If I speak in the tongues of men and of angels, but have not love, I am a noisy gong or a clanging cymbal" (1 Cor. 13:1). Most of us are immediately curious: What does Paul mean by the phrase "tongues of men and of angels"? The context suggests that he is speaking of the spiritual gift of tongues, something that was apparently highly valued by the Corinthian Christians. But what exactly does he mean by the two types of tongues mentioned here—of men and of angels? Just a few verses earlier, in a listing of the various gifts, Paul made a reference to "various kinds of tongues" (12:28). Could it be that here he is distinguishing further between earthly and heavenly languages, the latter being "a deluxe version"[1] of the gift?

Though we don't know the exact meaning behind this phrase, we do know that those who exercised this gift would have looked very spiritual to those who lacked the gift of speaking in tongues. Yet surprisingly, Paul does not emphasize the superior spirituality of those who speak in tongues. Instead, he says that those who speak in tongues of men—even tongues of angels—but who lack love are like a "noisy gong or a clanging cymbal."

The phrase "noisy gong" literally means "echoing bronze." The Greek city of Corinth, where the recipients of this letter lived, was famous for producing a special bronze alloy, and we know that cymbals were frequently used in their pagan worship. So Paul may be alluding to the godless, pagan worship of the city when he speaks of gifts exercised without love. In essence, he is telling the Corinthians that though speaking in tongues may appear spectacular and spiritual, without love it is no better than the practice of worshiping idols. There is plenty of noise and it looks impressive, but it's really just a waste of time![2]

Paul is implying, at the beginning of this chapter, that it is possible for people with prominent gifts of the Spirit to become void of Christlikeness. As he puts it, what matters are not the gifts themselves, but the love that guides their use. Paul assures the Corinthian Christians that apart from love, "I am nothing." It is all too easy for highly gifted people to find their identity and significance in their spiritual gifts and in the process lose the fruit of the Spirit, love.

A man or woman may have a burning desire to please God. So they begin to use their gifts in ministry and accomplish God's work in significant ways. Soon, however, their thirst for God is tragically replaced by a thirst for something else: recognition and success. Though they began working for God's glory, they have fallen into the trap of idolatry and have started seeking their own glory instead.

In the process, they become *unloving*.

At Christmastime in Sri Lanka, churches often put on various dramas and musical performances. Though the intent of this season is to honor Christ and celebrate his birth, many churches run into problems when they hand out parts in the dramas and musicals to the children. Parents grow angry when their child is not selected for a particular role or given an opportunity to sing. Their bitter reaction turns a time of celebration into a sour experience for other believers. I find it ironic that the celebration of an event marking the self-sacrificial love of Jesus is often marked by angry battles among his followers — bitter that they have not received something they wanted, something they felt they deserved!

Giftedness comes with many traps. When our gifts are not recognized by others, we can fall prey to temptation by growing angry and taking on the attitude of a victim. We begin to hustle for position and prominence, trying to draw attention to ourselves rather than using our God-given gifts to serve others.

Albert Orsborn (1886–1967) served for many years as the head of the Salvation Army and was its most famous hymn writer. As a young and successful officer in the Salvation Army, he grew angry over the decision of the leaders to split the region under his control into two separate sections. Orsborn found himself battling, not for the kingdom of God, but for his own position in the kingdom. Shortly after this happened, however, Orsborn was in an accident and found himself in the hospital for a lengthy season of recovery, a season that God used to powerfully bring him to repentance for his selfishness and back to Spirit-anointed usefulness.[3] In one of his hymns, he reflects on the lessons he learned during this time:

> Savior, if my feet have faltered
> On the pathway of the cross,
> If my purposes have altered
> Or my gold be mixed with dross,
> O forbid me not thy service,
> Keep me yet in thy employ,
> Pass me through a sterner cleansing
> If I may but give thee joy.[4]

Orsborn learned that the goal of his life, as a follower of Christ, was not satisfying his own personal ambition. Instead, God used his humiliation through weakness to help him grow into his true ambition in life — becoming more like Christ. Those who want to follow Christ must learn to be grateful for things that others consider setbacks, because the humbling of God helps us achieve our true ambition — loving service of others in the name of Christ.

PROPHECY, KNOWLEDGE AND FAITH

Next Paul writes, "And if I have prophetic powers, and understand all mysteries and all knowledge, and if I have all faith, so as to remove mountains, but have not love, I am nothing" (13:2). The gift of tongues was generally for personal edification, unless someone in the worship service translated a message given in tongues. Prophecy, by contrast, has a clear ministry to the church. So Paul says it is desirable to have people exercising it in the church (14:4 – 19). The context of verse 2 suggests that one who understands "all mysteries and all knowledge" has been given this ability as a gift of the Spirit.

The people described here can speak specifically to an individual's life, saying things that were not immediately evident to others. Some might use the gift to offer specific, divinely inspired direction to individuals or groups. Some would prophesy about the future. In 1 Corinthians 14 Paul clearly says that these gifts are desirable because they edify the church. Yet if the one who exercises these gifts does not have love, that person is "nothing."

"All faith, so as to remove mountains" probably refers to the gift of faith that is given to a few remarkable individuals (1 Cor. 12:9) rather than to saving faith, which is something that all Christians exercise. This is the faith that Peter had when he told the lame man, "In the name of Jesus Christ of Nazareth, rise up and walk!" (Acts 3:6). I often pray for the sick, believing that God can heal them. But I have never had the boldness to say something like what Peter and John said. I would say, "O Lord, heal this person." But Peter knew that God would miraculously raise up this lame man, and he told him to "rise up and walk."

Working on this plane, however, is strenuous. Sometimes people come up for prayer after a service, and I have the privilege of praying for them. After asking what it was that prompted them to come forward, I desperately ask God to give me the right words to pray, so that the prayer will align itself to God's will. At the end of such prayer sessions I sometimes find I am emotionally more exhausted than after I have preached. How much more would the strain be for those with a miraculous gift of discerning and applying God's will to situations. When a woman touched the hem of Jesus garment and was healed, Jesus inquired who had done this, "perceiving in himself that power had gone out from him" (Mark 5:30). So acting as a direct representative of God can be emotionally tiring. When we are emotionally exhausted, we can become irritable with our colleagues and family. Sadly, some public figures are not pleasant company to those who are intimate with them.

The miraculous gift of faith can also be seen in the faith of daring pioneers who believe God for the impossible. These are men and women who dream great dreams, build organizations, and develop programs that serve those in need. James Hudson Taylor had a daring vision that led him to start China Inland Mission (now called OMF International). As a young man I recall reading an inspiring book, *A Passion for the Impossible*, that described the history of this movement.[5] Thankfully, Hudson Taylor was not an impatient man and was willing to pursue his vision for the sake of love rather than for immediate results.

Sadly, however, many of today's visionaries have great faith in God, but they are impatient with and sometimes unkind to colleagues. On the day of a huge program they organized, you may find them speaking harshly to a person who made a mistake or was responsible for something that went wrong. Humanly speaking the program was a great success. Can we describe the chief organizer of that program as "nothing"? After all, this program was his vision; he carried it to a successful completion through his amazing faith. How can you call a person like that "nothing"? Yet from the perspective of Paul, even though the program was a roaring success, the director of the program was an absolute failure ("nothing").

The person whom Paul calls "nothing" in this passage is the one who "understands all mysteries and all knowledge" and has "all faith." Three times he uses the word "all" to indicate how advanced and seemingly mature this person is in the life of service. Most likely, this person is a prominent leader with significant gifts, someone who is ministering publicly and seeing visible results. But here, we learn that they are *nothing*!

This helps us to reformulate our definition of success. Far too often, gifted but ungodly people are given positions of influence in the church. When their character is revealed and the fruit of selfishness and sin becomes apparent, it can bring great shame to the church. Sadly, the history of the church is ridden with stories of abuse, war, revenge, brutality, injustice, internal strife, and division because gifted people did not have the corresponding character of Christ.

We are inclined to ignore problems that we might see in the personal life of a prominent person. We may notice that they tend to neglect their relationship with their family or wife, but we see great results in their public ministry. It's easy to ignore such problems when that ministry is "successful" and people are coming to know Christ. We overlook those issues because we know that if that person were to step down from public ministry in order to straighten out his personal life, the church or the organization would suffer. We fear that attendance would drop and donations to the ministry would decrease.

We are all vulnerable here. Few people see into our private lives, nor are they aware of the intimate details of our walk with God. Sometimes our family members will know the truth of the matter, but they will not generally betray us in public. As followers of Christ, we must reject the temptation to allow our public image and actions to compromise our inner life. If we must sacrifice our prominence, a promotion, our earthly significance, or worldly opportunities to use our gifts, let us gladly make the sacrifice!

But when it comes to our relationship with God, it is better to be safe and deprive ourselves of an apparent blessing than to be sorry that we went down the wrong path. We must remember that it is, in fact, no sacrifice at all to deprive ourselves of an earthly honor for the sake of God's love. A life rooted in the love of God is a happy life. The source of happiness is something that the world cannot touch. So we can be deprived but happy. What greater wealth is there in the world than happiness—the joy of knowing the love and approval of God!

CHAPTER 2

GREATER THAN RADICAL COMMITMENT

1 CORINTHIANS 13:3

IN THE FIRST THREE VERSES of 1 Corinthians 13 Paul is showing us that many things Christians regard as things of great value are useless without love. He first listed some of the more spectacular gifts given by God (13:1–2). Now, in verse 3, he mentions two actions that we commonly associate with a radical commitment to God: giving of our possessions and giving of one's life.

It's clear from reading the New Testament that one of the clearest tests of a person's commitment to God is whether that commitment has gone down to his wallet. Jesus told the rich man that if he wished to be perfect, he should sell all that he had and follow him (Matt. 19:21; Luke 18:22). Yet 1 Corinthians 13:3 Paul tells us that there is something even more fundamental than radical giving. He writes: "If I give away all I have … but have not love, I gain nothing" (13:3). Radical giving—even giving away all that we have—means nothing if it lacks love.

When we first read this, we may wonder: "How can we give at that level of sacrifice and yet still lack love? How is that even possible?" I can think of at least seven ways in which it is possible to give sacrificially—without having genuine love.

GIVING SACRIFICIALLY—WITHOUT LOVE

1. GIVING FOR MERIT

In Sri Lanka, I will often encounter beggars who say, "May you attain merit," when they are requesting alms or gifts of charity. According to the majority religions in Sri Lanka, our actions (or karma) determine our destiny in our next life. When some Sri Lankans ask for help, they believe that they are doing you a favor by giving you an opportunity to affect your destiny. At the root of it all is an assumption that our gifts to others somehow *earn* us favor.

Sadly, a similar mind-set is rampant in the church today. We often hear people telling others that if they give generously, they will be blessed and will prosper. I once saw an advertisement inviting people to invest in "blessing shares" in a Christian organization. A gift to this organization was viewed as an investment that would lead to divine blessings for the giver.

The Bible does, indeed, tell us that God will bless those who give generously and sacrificially. In 2 Corinthians 9:6, Paul wrote, "Whoever sows sparingly will also reap sparingly, and whoever sows bountifully will also reap bountifully." The reason the Bible presents this reality is to encourage us amidst the seeming folly of following the way of the cross.

Though many say it is foolish to be generous, that is not the case. To use a metaphor that Jesus used, generosity is actually a smart investment in heaven, where there is no corruption and loss through robbery. Today we could say, where there is no inflation and other economic uncertainties (see Matt. 6:20). *Yet, though blessings are promised by God, the Bible never holds out personal financial gain as the primary motive for our generosity.*

2. GIVING OUT OF A SENSE OF DUTY

There is no beauty in duty if it is done solely out of obligation. Dutiful people may be considered "good" people, but they can easily make goodness appear unattractive, especially if they do the right things but have anger, bitterness, or a judgmental attitude toward others. A judgmental attitude can make it unpleasant to be around them. If you have a tough job to do, such as caring for a sick parent or a severely handicapped child, it is necessary to guard against this temptation. Be sure to check your heart and seek to be grounded in the love of God, praying that he will help you to graduate from duty to love. We will talk more about this later when we discuss kindness in chapter 6. At this point, we simply want to remember that acts of radical sacrifice, even those done out of a sense of duty, can be meaningless if they lack love.

3. GIVING TO AVOID GETTING INVOLVED

Sometimes we give a person something that may not meet his or her real need. We give to them because we know that our money or our gift will get rid of them. A friend may ask us for financial help, but what he really *needs* is some guidance and training on how to budget wisely. We recognize that this will require a commitment we are unable or unwilling to make, and so we give him some money instead. In many ways, this is what we do when we give money to someone on the street who suffers from an addiction to alcohol or drugs. Our gift satisfies a temporary need for them, but it compounds the deeper problem of their addiction.

We should acknowledge that it is not humanly possible for us to meet every need we encounter. We must use godly wisdom to decide what needs we can actually commit to meet. At times, we may give something, though that may not be the best long-term way to help that person. I admit that I often do this with beggars who ask for help. Rarely am I 100 percent certain that they have a genuine need. I confess that I do not have the time to commit myself to finding out. Thus I give a little, hoping that it will help the person out in a limited way. In others cases, we may decide not to help at all.

There is no right answer here. Again, the key issue we must resolve is the question of our motive: *Are we giving to avoid getting involved, or are we motivated by love for the person?* At times, genuine love may lead us to give, while at other times, it may lead us *not* to give.

4. GIVING WHEN WE SHOULD NOT GIVE

Henry Drummond (1851 – 1897) was a Scottish evangelist, theologian, and scientist who wrote a little book on 1 Corinthians 13 in 1874 called *The Greatest Thing in the World*. The book was popular in his day, and it continues to be reprinted today. In his book, Drummond observes that "love is just as often in the withholding."[1] When appropriate, love says "no." At times, love may mean *not* giving a person what they have requested. If you are a parent, you have likely seen what happens to children who cry out loud enough and long enough until their parents give them what they want merely to silence them. Those children develop an unhealthy pattern of belief: that if they cry out loud enough and long enough, they will ultimately get what they want.

Loving parents know that they must withhold things from their children, even when it means enduring the pain of hearing them cry. Children who grow up learning to live with the "no" they receive from their parents will come to respect them as people who are firm in their decisions, particularly when given in the context of loving discipline and godly correction. If the parents are reasonable in their refusals, the children will feel secure as they grow because they know that their parents are strong, stable, and unswerving. Children who feel they can get what they want by crying loud enough will eventually lose respect for their parents. That is why a firm "no" is a major factor in nurturing a secure child.

The patterns parents establish with their children also have consequences for their lives as Christians. Children whose parents wavered in saying "yes" and "no" will find it difficult when they have to say "no" to the things they desire as young adults. When those children become Christians, they will find it difficult to crucify the flesh and surrender things that are not helpful to them. They have never learned to say "no" and must discipline and train themselves in denying the things that are not good or conducive to their growth in Christ.

One of the secret joys in the Christian life is learning to surrender. Good things can rob us of our joy as Christians because they get in the way of better things. You surrender sleep in order to visit a troubled friend or surrender an enjoyable television program in order to talk to your troubled spouse. But if you grow up with a healthy attitude to surrendering things for your own good, you can happily give them up. Let's nurture people who learn to respect the word "no."

5. GIVING WITHOUT IDENTIFYING WITH THOSE WE SERVE

Many people who help the poor financially are content to do so from a comfortable distance. This is why often social workers are resented by those they help. Those who receive help are often made to feel inferior by the attitude and actions of those helping them. Our method should be that of Jesus, who "made himself nothing, taking the form of a servant, being born in the likeness of men" (Phil. 2:7). Sometimes after a huge disaster workers will not have time to get too close to those whom they help because of the massive amount of work that has to be done immediately. But they still can go with an attitude of humble servanthood. During the relief operation in Sri Lanka following the terrible tsunami of December 2004, many people commented about how kind the Christians had been to them; often it was the humble spirit and friendliness of the helpers that impressed them the most.

In Christianity the model that perpetuates the donor-receiver mentality has been replaced with the model of partnership. The daughter church in Antioch, for example, sent funds to the mother church in Jerusalem, which had sent the gospel to Antioch (Acts 11:28–30). They became partners together in God's mission.

I have worked primarily with the poor for most of my life. The organization and church I am part of have helped many economically. But I cannot feel superior to them because there is so much I can learn from them. Not having much, they are forced to be more dependent on God for everything. They have taught me about vibrantly praying through their attitude of dependence. I also have learned about generosity from them, because despite their poverty they are so eager to help others when there is a need.

I believe prayer is more important than money in carrying out the mission of the church. The one who gives money cannot think that he or she is superior to the one who prays. Through identification we must foster this understanding of a partnership of equals as soon as possible when working with economically needy persons.

6. GIVING FOR RECOGNITION

Earlier, we saw that there is a danger in giving to earn merit from God. Closely associated with this is the desire to give so that we gain recognition from others. Jesus said "Beware of practicing your righteousness before other people to be seen by them, for then you will have no reward from your Father who is in heaven.... But when you give to the needy, do not let your left hand know what your right hand is doing, so that your giving may be in secret" (Matt. 6:1, 3–4). Churches and organizations sometimes present the prospect of publicity and recognition as an incentive to giving. You can find advertisements promising that if you give to a certain cause, your name will appear in that magazine, or a special plaque recognizing your gift will be displayed somewhere in a building.

We easily forget that giving is not some great achievement. Everything we have belongs to God. After the people of Israel had given willingly and sacrificially toward the temple, in David's prayer on their behalf he freely acknowledged that they had done *nothing* special in their giving: "But who am I, and what is my people, that we should be able thus to offer willingly? For all things come from you, and *of your own* have we given you" (1 Chron. 29:14, emphasis added). We must remember that giving is not some great achievement on our part. In all of our giving we never come close to repaying the debt of love we owe Christ, who "though he was rich, yet for [our] sake he became poor, so that [we] by his poverty might become rich" (2 Cor. 8:9).

When the Bible does recognize the gifts and sacrifices that others make, it does so to provide an example for us to follow. We tend to highlight large donations, which we believe will eliminate poverty and lead to spectacular results, when it is really the gifts of the poor that should be recognized because they are so sacrificial and costly. When Jesus chose to highlight generous giving, he drew attention to the very small gift of the widow, who "put in two small copper coins, which make a penny," because "she out of her poverty has put in everything she had, all she had to live on" (Mark 12:42, 44). Paul chose to highlight the gift of the Macedonians because "in a severe test of affliction, their abundance of joy and their extreme poverty have overflowed in a wealth of generosity on their part" (2 Cor. 8:2). In both of these situations, it was the act of sacrificial generosity—rooted in love—that was highlighted, not the giver. When those who give seek publicity or recognition through the gifts they give, they are falling short of the Christian model of loving.

7. GIVING WITH A COMPETITIVE SPIRIT

In a small town in Asia there is a small population of Christians and two church buildings that belong to two different denominations. Both of these buildings look similar, and they were both built through the gifts of two wealthy brothers, brothers who were often angry with each other and regularly competed with one another. Today, they stand not as a testimony of Christian love, but as a testimony to the power of competition.

The Bible teaches us to give based on the standard of loving concern for the needs of others, out of the overflow of our heart, and not for selfish ambition or out of a competitive spirit. We are asked to decide how much we should give based on an evaluation of the person's need (2 Cor. 8:14) and on how God has blessed us financially (Deut. 16:10; 1 Cor. 16:2).

These are just a few examples that show us that it is indeed possible to give generously, sacrificially, and spectacularly—all that we have—yet miss the mark. First Corinthians 13:3 reminds us that there is something more essential to our giving than the amount or the level of sacrifice. All giving, even that which is marked by generosity and sacrifice, must be motivated by love. "If I give away all I have … but have not love, I gain nothing."

MARTYRDOM OR PHYSICAL HARDSHIP

Paul's list of "useless" things climaxes with what most would consider as the supreme act of service and devotion to God: martyrdom. He says, " … if I deliver up my body to be burned, but have not love, I gain nothing" (1 Cor. 13:3b). First, I should point out that there is some uncertainty about the original language in this verse, whether it should be translated as being burned or in the most general sense of hardship (e.g., NIV: "and give over my body to hardship that I may boast"). The NIV adds the words "to hardship" as an explanatory addition, even though they are not in the original Greek; but regardless of the exact translation, it is evident that Paul is talking about physical sacrifice, even to the point of death.

In the early church martyrdom had become such a symbol of honor that "some rushed to martyrdom wanting the glory of it." As Gerald Sittser observes, "They bore witness to themselves more than they bore witness to the gospel." As a result "early Christian leaders [had] to establish standards for martyrdom, so that those only who were called to it, against their natural wishes, were given the title 'martyr.'"[2] People can make sacrifices with the aim of receiving personal glory through it.

Sometimes Christians could grow bitter over a price they have paid through a heroic commitment to a project that led to exhaustion, injury, sickness, and even death. They may grumble about their lot. They will blame others for not helping them, for not providing relief to them, or for not working as hard as they have worked. They may grow angry with those who have caused them to suffer.

There are some who have been persecuted for their faith, but they are not happy about it. They have suffered mental wounds that have been caused by physical wounds, wounds that hurt long after the physical wounds have healed. I have spoken to faithful Christians who have been persecuted for their faith and heard them express bitterness over the way they were treated years earlier.

Not only is it humiliating to be physically hit or beaten; it also takes time to heal. We will look at how we should respond to this type of persecution in greater detail later in this book in our discussions about patience, anger, and endurance. But we must hold on to the promise that the love of

God can and does heal the wounds that we suffer in the name of Christ. Stephen demonstrated the power of the love of Christ when he cried out as he was being stoned to death: "Lord, do not hold this sin against them" (Acts 7:60). Stephen had earlier had a vision of Christ (7:56), and this vision gave him the strength to experience the fellowship of sharing in Christ's suffering, enabling the love of God within him to continue to burn even as he experienced the brutality of the enemy.

Sadly, as Paul suggests in 1 Corinthians 13:3, even deeply dedicated Christians may lack love in the face of persecution and great physical sacrifice. He tells us that those who give their bodies (either to the flames or to boasting) without love "gain nothing" (13:3). Suicide bombers go on their expeditions of hate, expecting a martyr's paradise. But they are mistaken. Great sacrifice, done in hatred, does not accomplish anything of ultimate value and worth. It is only when our sacrifice draws attention to the power and beauty of the love of God that we see the true value of sacrificial love.

, , ,

Before the practice of apartheid was abolished in South Africa, Benjamin Dube was hated by many extremists among his own people because he preached a message of love rather than hatred toward his "enemies." At one point, Benjamin called his family together and told them that he had been threatened and would probably soon be killed. "Remain faithful to Jesus," he told them; "love those who will kill me—because Jesus loves them."

Some time later while driving his car, Dube was stopped by a mob, dragged from his vehicle, and beaten to death. His Bible was later found beside him, drenched in his blood.

With him in the car was his twelve-year-old son, Benjamin Jr., who somehow managed to escape from the murderous gang. Hiding behind a barrel, the boy witnessed what the mob had done to his father. Benjamin ran home, told his mother what had happened, went to his room, and wept all through the night.

As he wept, he heard a wonderful voice speaking to him. His mother, Grace, who relates this story, does not explain more about that voice. Benjamin's father had often told him, "Benjamin, you must take my place to sing for the Lord if anything happens to me." Early the next morning, his mother, Grace, heard her son singing. At first it was a broken voice, but then, the song grew clearer and stronger. He was singing a song from Scripture: "Father forgive them, for they do not know what they are doing."

Grace and Benjamin Jr. frequently sang that song in the days and weeks after that horrible event. Years later, they sang it again at a meeting in their hometown of Soweto. After singing, Grace went on to speak about forgiving a sinning brother seventy-seven times (Matt. 18:21–22).

After the meeting a man came up to her looking scared and ashamed. After being prompted by Grace to say what was bothering him, the man confessed to her, "I need your Jesus, I need forgiveness. I ... I was one of the mob who killed your husband." Like Corrie ten Boom, Grace, too, experienced a moment of hesitancy. But soon the power of God's love won through in her own heart. She put her arms around the killer, forgave him for killing her husband, and whispered to him, "You are now my brother."[3]

While there are examples of those who make great sacrifices without love, there are also many examples of those who demonstrate the power of Christian love by the way they sacrificed for God. The presence of Christ with them enables them to face their trials without losing their joy and peace and to keep on loving people, even those who hurt them.

CHAPTER 3

PATIENCE WITH WEAKNESSES
1 CORINTHIANS 13:4A

NOW THAT PAUL has demonstrated the priority and uniqueness of love as the quality that, by its presence, gives lasting, eternal value to our use of God's gifts, our acts of generosity, and our acts of radical sacrifice, he proceeds to list some of the unique characteristics of this love. Rather than using adjectives to describe the uniqueness of love, however, he uses fifteen verbs over four verses (1 Cor. 13:4–7).[1] As biblical scholar David Garland suggests, Paul appears to be emphasizing the active and decisive character of Christian love: "Love is dynamic and active, not something static. He is not talking about some inner feeling or emotion. Love is not conveyed by words; it has to be shown. It can only be defined by what it does and does not do."[2]

It may be significant that the first verb Paul chooses to describe love is "to be patient." This is significant because the Greek verb we translate "is patient," along with its corresponding noun ("patience"), appear fifteen times in the New Testament to describe the character of believers. In addition, it is used six times to describe the character of God's attitude toward us. In his list of the fruit of the Spirit, patience is mentioned after the familiar triad of love, joy, and peace. Obviously, patience is an important characteristic of Christian love, but it is also something that most Christians find difficult to demonstrate in their lives. Perhaps that is why it is mentioned so often! In fact, there is so much to say about patience that I have split this material into three chapters. I can honestly say that trying to help Christians learn to be patient has been one of the most difficult challenges I have faced in my ministry of discipleship.

The Greek word Paul uses here (*makrothymeō*) generally refers to patience that is extended toward people. In past centuries, it was translated into the old English as "suffereth long" or long-suffering (KJV; see "suffers wrong" NKJV). A different word (*hypomenō*) is usually translated as "endures" and appears in verse 7. That word is typically used in connection with trials.[3] As we consider our need for patience with people, I find it is possible to talk about several different ways of showing this aspect of Christian love to others. However, many of these ways can be summarized into two broad categories: showing patience when dealing with the weaknesses of other people, and showing patience when dealing with the sins of people. In this chapter, we will look at what it means to be patient with weaknesses, and in the next chapter we will discuss the need for patience when dealing with sin.

PATIENCE WITH WEAKNESSES

In 1 Thessalonians 5:14, Paul writes, "And we urge you, brothers, admonish the idle, encourage the fainthearted, help the weak, *be patient with them all*" (emphasis added). We all have weaknesses. Some of these are not easy to change. There are weaknesses that are part of our personality, part of our unique makeup as individuals. And there are some weaknesses that are due to different experiences we have had in life, experiences that have been negative and have left wounds or shaped us in an unhealthy way.

In Romans 8:26 Paul uses graphic language to describe how the Holy Spirit comes to us and helps us with our weaknesses: "Likewise the Spirit helps us in our weakness. For we do not know what to pray for as we ought, but the Spirit himself intercedes for us with groanings too deep for words." The word "helps" in this passage is actually a much longer word in the Greek (*synantilambanomai*), which combines three words together. It literally means "takes share in." A commentator from an earlier generation, A. T. Robertson, explains that this word reminds us that even though our weaknesses can seem like a huge burden — like a log that we struggle to carry — the Holy Spirit comes alongside us and "takes share in" our struggle and suffering. He helps us to bear the weight of the burden we carry.[4] This reflects his role as our counselor and comforter. The Greek word used to describe this is *parakletos,* which literally means "one who is called to someone's aid."[5]

Romans 8:26 goes on to say that the Holy Spirit "intercedes for us with groanings too deep for words." We groan with our weaknesses (see 8:23), and the Spirit comes so close to us in identifying with our need for help that our groans become his. In other words, we have a God who *understands* our weaknesses. As Hebrews 4:15 tells us, "For we do not have a high priest who is unable to sympathize with our weaknesses, but one who in every respect has been tempted as we are, yet without sin."

One of my most embarrassing experiences in life came when I was about five years old and was attending a family camp. My stomach was upset, and though I tried hard to find a rest room, I could not make it in time. I still remember crying out, in pain and embarrassment, "My God, my God, why have you forsaken me!" Fifty years later, as I struggled to come to terms with the terrible destruction and pain caused by the tsunami that hit India and Sri Lanka in December 2004, I recalled that experience, how I had first uttered those words in my utter embarrassment. Though I had heard them repeated many times, I was reminded in a profound way that these are words spoken by Jesus himself. They are the words of someone feeling the pain of my embarrassment as well as the heartache of suffering destruction and abandonment.

I find hope in knowing we have a God who understands our struggle with weaknesses and patiently comes near to us to help us. And those of us who have experienced his comfort must be willing to get close to those who struggle with weaknesses and be patient with them.

WEAKNESSES THAT ARE PART OF OUR PERSONALITY

As I mentioned earlier, some weaknesses are simply a part of our personality, our unique makeup. They are not matters of sin, though they can lead to sinful behavior if not disciplined. Some people are careless by nature, while others are scatterbrained. Some are slow and deliberative about the way they go about life while others are fast and impulsive. I find it amusing to observe what happens when a slow person marries a fast person—it certainly makes for an interesting marriage!

These types of weaknesses are not going to leave us this side of heaven. Patience is needed in dealing with weaknesses, particularly when we are dealing with the weaknesses of people who are close to us, and those weaknesses are closely related to values that are important to us. For example, I have a friend in ministry who married a lady who shares his burden for doing ministry, and she has been a wonderful partner for him in this regard. At the same time, my friend likes to keep a neat and tidy house. Unfortunately, his wife does not share this desire with him. He immediately notices when something is out of place, but she is not inclined that way—in the least!

Frequently we must enter into partnerships with people who are very different from us. We marry a person, and that relationship is for life. We have roommates, colleagues, business partners, team members, and fellow church members, and we must learn to get along with them, despite our different personalities. We may take on the responsibility to disciple or to be discipled by someone. We have elderly parents who become like children in their need for care. We may have people close to us who suffer from psychological disorders. Each one of these people will have certain qualities that annoy us. Nevertheless, we still have a relationship with these people, a relationship that we cannot simply cancel or end because we find things about them that annoy us.

We agree to accept a person into a relationship "for better, for worse," as the wording of the marriage service puts it. And we should learn to accept the fact that this person with whom we relate may not get rid of their weaknesses overnight ... as long as they live on earth. We exercise love toward them by dealing with them patiently. We decide that we will not make a big deal out of their personality quirks and differences. We choose not to harp on them, constantly nagging or asking them to change. If the person is ashamed of a weakness, we do not even need to bring it up.

There are times when my wife gets on my nerves. What do I do? I sometimes go to my room and grit my teeth. I once jokingly told her that I won't know what to do when I'm older and have lost all of my teeth. I do this because I know that there is no point in exploding over a relatively inconsequential thing that annoys me. The truth is that there are many things that I admire about my wife that far outweigh her weaknesses. What folly, then, to focus on the weaknesses! We must learn to find a way to handle the weaknesses of others and then get on with the business of loving and enjoying the other person.

In a passage appealing for unity in the church, Paul says that in humility we should "count others more significant than [ourselves]" (Phil. 2:3). Paul is not asking us to falsely act, as if other people are superior to us in every way when we know, in fact, that they are not. Everyone has something, some area or skill or gift that God has given to them in which they are better than us. Paul is asking us to focus our attention on those things. In eight of his thirteen letters, Paul includes specific things for which he thanks God, listing some of the good things he sees in the lives of his recipients. Focusing on the good we see in others gives us a good context for working together. This means that in every relationship we have a decision to make. What will we choose to focus on? Love for a person will lead us to focus on things that make us glad about the person, things we can celebrate about them.

I once stayed in a home in India in which the youngest of three sons had Down's syndrome. I noticed that he had a beautiful relationship with his elder brother. When I was talking to this brother, he told me of different ways in which his younger brother (the one with Down's) was an example to him. Instead of focusing on his brother's weaknesses, he had made a decision to focus on his brother's good qualities and to enjoy them.

But what about the disadvantages that come along with our weaknesses? As we seek to love another person, we should examine ways in which we can continue in the relationship, despite the weaknesses.

We will try to help the person to improve in weak areas. I am forgetful, so I had to learn to write down everything I have to do. It was helpful to have others remind me of this or encourage me in this area.

We will work out ways in which the work gets done despite the weakness of the person. This often means having someone else take over responsibilities in the areas the person is weak in. My friend whose wife was not good at keeping a neat house decided that he would take on that responsibility instead. In the Scriptures, we see that God gave Aaron to Moses as a spokesman when Moses protested that he could not speak well.

We may need to move a person to an area or a ministry where his weakness will not appear as evident to others. For example, I would never attempt to work in a job that involves keeping accounts or adding and subtracting because I am terrible with numbers. If I were required to work in an accounting job, even compensating for my weaknesses would not help. The most loving thing to do would be to reassign me into another department!

WEAKNESSES BECAUSE OF EXPERIENCES WE HAVE HAD

Some people's weaknesses are part of their personality, as we have seen, but others are related to experiences they have had in life. With these types of weakness there is a better chance of healing, as God's grace can be applied to that experience. This calls for a patient person who is willing to see the person through to the completion of the healing process, even though often scars may remain. Our constructive patience in dealing with wounded people can be God's means of bringing healing to them.

The power of patient love in bringing God's healing grace to our weaknesses can be seen in many different ways. A young man, who had adolescent sexual experiences that were too intense for him at that age, grows up with abnormally strong sexual desires that he finds difficult to control. He needs the patient care of knowledgeable people to help him find freedom. Childhood experiences like injustice or rejection can often leave people with weaknesses that cause them to erupt in anger later in life.

Or consider a young man who is bothered when he discovers that his fiancée is unresponsive when he touches her. Yet he refuses to reject her because of this. As they talk further about this problem, he learns that she was sexually abused as a child. Because of that experience, she has grown to have ambivalent feelings about the touch of a man. Once the young man finds this out, he is able to locate a counselor who can help her to find healing from her wounds. He patiently walks through the process with her. Because of the healing she experiences in the counseling and thanks to the young man's patience with his fiancée, they are able to enter into marriage with the strong likelihood of having a healthy sexual relationship.

In 1983 we had a terrible riot in my homeland of Sri Lanka. This event became the trigger that transformed a long-standing ethnic conflict between the Tamil and the Sinhala ethnic groups into a full-blown war. The house of a young man who had recently become a follower of Christ through our ministry was burned and completely destroyed in those riots. He was from the minority Tamil race, while I am from the majority Sinhala race. After his home was destroyed, this young man came to our home with his Hindu mother and remained with us for about six months. During this time he became like a son to me. His mother, sister, and brother also came to Christ within that year.

As the war progressed, Tamil militants often set off bombs in public places in our city. Whenever that happened, it incited fear and inflamed ethnic hatred. Suddenly, all the Tamil young people became suspects. At various checkpoints throughout the city, they would be stopped and interrogated. Some were arrested. These were difficult times for the Tamil youth—especially the Tamil youth who had rejected violence as a means of getting their rights. Though they had rejected violence, they were still treated as terrorists.

The young man I had welcomed into our home occasionally would call me and scold me because as a result of our relationship, he had developed a love for our nation and for those of the Sinhala race. But now he felt terrible being treated like a traitor to his nation, having done nothing wrong. Because he had no one else to talk to, he often scolded me and took out his frustration on me for the suffering and mistreatment he was experiencing. Rather than responding in kind, I took it as a privilege to be the recipient of his scolding, though it was not always easy to hear him say things about my own race and the nation that I love. I tried to be an agent of healing in his life by patiently listening to and empathizing with his legitimate expressions of anger.

, , ,

We live in a world whose warped values see weak and unproductive people as unimportant. It seems like a waste of time to invest time and energy in such people. But the way a Christian views people is radically different. We know that on the day of judgment, God will not be concerned with our worldly accomplishments. He will look at the fruit of our faith in Jesus Christ—how we treated the hungry, the thirsty, the stranger, the naked, the sick, and the prisoner (Matt. 25:35–36), people whom our society regards as weak and unproductive.

While the world values success and applauds those who are driven by selfish ambition, we follow a different set of values. Paul told the Ephesian elders, "In all things I have shown you that by working hard in this way we must help the weak" (Acts 20:35). The greatest of the apostles worked hard. Why? *To help the weak!* In our throwaway society such activity looks like a waste of time. Is it any wonder that the church is so shallow when we shun the opportunities God gives us to help weak people? Instead, we must learn to be patient in dealing with the weaknesses of others.

CHAPTER 4

PATIENCE WITH SIN
1 CORINTHIANS 13:4A

A PASTOR FRIEND of mine went to visit an old lady who was unable to attend church in order to administer the Lord's Supper to her. During their conversation she told him, "Pastor, one thing you must not ask me to do is to forgive my sister. That, I cannot do!" In the previous chapter we looked at how Christians respond with patience in connection with people's weaknesses. This lady's attitude highlights the need for another aspect of patience: the willingness to forgive those who sin against us. In this chapter we will look at how we can do this and overcome the obstacles to forgiveness.

A RESPONSE TO HOW GOD DEALS WITH US

The Christian practice of being patient with those who sin against us is rooted in our experience of God having had patience with us. Peter says, "The Lord ... is patient toward you, not wishing that any should perish, but that all should reach repentance" (2 Peter 3:9; see also 1 Peter 3:20; 2 Peter 3:15). Paul saw the miracle of his conversion, after being "the foremost" of sinners, as a striking example of God's patience. He writes, "But I received mercy for this reason, that in me, as the foremost, Jesus Christ might display his perfect patience as an example to those who were to believe in him for eternal life" (1 Tim. 1:16). Those who have tasted the amazing grace of God and know that they have been shown mercy should be the first to recognize that God has been patient toward them, not treating them as their sins deserve.

In the New Testament, the verb and the noun for patience occur six different times to describe God's patience with us.[1] Our salvation is entirely due to the grace and mercy of God, who "shows his love for us in that while we were still sinners, Christ died for us" (Rom. 5:8). Each of us has committed a grave and serious sin; we have rebelled against the Lord of the universe in an act of treason, declaring that we are unwilling to live under his gracious government. Yet he forgives us when we come to him in repentance.

Even after receiving such amazing forgiveness, we continue to sin against him. And each time we return to him in repentance, God forgives us. Knowing that God responds to our sins with such patience and forgiveness helps us to show patience toward others when they sin against us. This is what Jesus taught his disciples when he taught them to ask for God's forgiveness — "forgive us our debts [sins]" — adding, "as we also have forgiven our debtors" (Matt. 6:12). Jesus continued: "For if you forgive others their trespasses, your heavenly Father will also forgive you, but if you do not forgive others their trespasses, neither will your Father forgive your trespasses" (Matt. 6:14–15). On another occasion, in response to a question about the number of times we should forgive a brother, Jesus said we should forgive them even as much as "seventy-seven times," which indicates that there should be, in effect, no limit to our willingness to forgive.

Jesus went on to tell the story of a servant who had been forgiven a huge debt, yet refused to forgive his fellow servant a much smaller debt (Matt. 18:22–34). The unforgiving servant received a severe punishment for his unwillingness to forgive those who owed him, after receiving abundant grace in his own life. Jesus concluded the story: "So also my heavenly Father will do to every one of you, if you do not forgive your brother from your heart" (Matt. 18:35). Clearly, God expects that those who have been forgiven will be willing to forgive those who sin against them. In addition to remembering the grace that God has shown us in the gospel, we should also remember the corresponding seriousness with which God treats our failure to forgive.

In his letter to the Colossian church, Paul wrote: "Put on then ... patience, bearing with one another and, if one has a complaint against another, forgiving each other; as the Lord has forgiven you, so you also must forgive" (Col. 3:12–13). Again, our patience with others is presented as a response to God's forgiving us. And after asking Timothy to "reprove, rebuke, and exhort"—all things that are necessary to do when someone has sinned—Paul concludes his advice to Timothy by adding that all of this must be done "with complete *patience* and teaching" (2 Tim. 4:2, emphasis mine). Peter agrees with this in his own letter: "Above all, keep loving one another earnestly, since love covers a multitude of sins" (1 Peter 4:8).

In many of our cultures, forgiving or being patient with those who sin against us is regarded as a violation of family honor. I have found that with some converts to Christianity, trying to persuade people not to take revenge is a hard task. That seems to go against values of right and wrong ingrained in the minds of these new converts. We must inform them of the corresponding seriousness before God of a failure to forgive.

HOW CAN WE LOVE AFTER SO MUCH HURT?

But this raises a question for many people: How can we love after so much hurt? I don't want to just dismiss this question, as it is an expression of very real pain. The Bible is sensitive to the pain of injustice and the reality that we are often hurt deeply by the sins of others. We all can recognize when something wrong has been done to us or to others, and we have an innate sense that such actions should be punished.

This sense of justice is an instinct that can be traced back to our creation in the image of God, and it is a good gift of God. In the Psalms, we see godly people giving vent to their rage over the hurt done to them. They reflect the just character of God and his hatred of sin when they revolt in anger against wrongs committed. A large number of psalms are called laments because they are actually complaints to God as people mourn over their suffering despite the fact that they have been righteous and faithful to him. Some of these psalms are called imprecatory psalms: they call curses on those who have done wrong to them.

What a relief it is to have such psalms in the Bible! These passages of Scripture show us that deep feelings of hurt and revolt over wrongs committed against us are natural and normal. Psalms like these can also have a sobering influence on those of us who are trying to minister to hurting people. They remind us that we need to be sensitive to the hurts people have and to avoid simplistic solutions to their pain.

Antoine Rutayisire, a church leader from Rwanda who lost many of his loved ones in the Rwandan genocide, is now actively involved in bringing healing to his land. During a visit he made to Sri Lanka I talked with him about the difficult task of leading people who have been deeply wounded to forgive those who have hurt them. Antoine shared that caution is needed in many of these cases. He said that it can be damaging to try forcing people to forgive those who have hurt them before they are ready for it. To glibly tell deeply hurt people to forgive communicates to them that we aren't taking the wrong that was done to them seriously. We must remember that God is a God of justice, and there are consequences to sin. This means that we must never downplay the seriousness of wrongdoing or sinful behavior. We must remember that it was precisely because sin was so serious that God's own Son had to die a painful death on a Roman cross to win our forgiveness.

In the next chapter we will look more closely at how we can learn to love wrongdoers without compromising justice. But for now, I want simply to emphasize that we must exercise caution when we approach hurting people. As we seek to help them, we should cultivate an attitude that is sensitive to the wrongness of the hurts they have experienced. If we begin with an honest acknowledgment of their hurt and then help them bring that pain to God in the form of a lament, this openness about their pain and the wrong that was done to them can unlock the door to God's comfort and healing. And though the process of healing may be long and complex, somewhere in this process there must be a place for forgiving and loving those who hurt us.

TWO POWERFUL TRUTHS
GOD'S LOVE IS GREATER THAN WICKEDNESS

There are two powerful truths that give us the strength to forgive and love those who have wronged us. The first truth is that we have strength to love because *God's love is greater than all the wrongdoing in the world.* Earlier, we referred to Romans 5:5: "God's love has been poured into our hearts through the Holy Spirit who has been given to us." We said that this verse indicates that God's love is an inexhaustible resource coming from his eternal reservoir. This divine love is greater than all the wickedness and unkindness a human could face.

Corrie ten Boom, whom we read about in the introduction, struggled with bitterness when she was in the concentration camp. She writes, "Sometimes bitterness and hatred tried to enter my heart when people were so cruel to my sister and me. Then," she went on to say, "I learned this prayer, a 'thank you' for Romans 5:5." This was her prayer: "Thank you, Lord Jesus, that you have brought into my heart the love of God through the Holy Spirit, who is given to me. Thank you, Father, that your love in me is victorious over the bitterness in me and the cruelty around me." Corrie writes that after she prayed this prayer, "I experienced the miracle that there was no room for bitterness in my heart anymore."[2]

Corrie ten Boom shares of another time when her sister Betsie was too sick and weak to do the work of shoveling dirt that the guards were forcing them to do. Corrie remembers one of the guards poking fun at how little dirt there was in her sister's shovel. As a result, many of the guards and even some of the prisoners laughed along as they teased Betsie. When Betsie tried to explain that she was too weak to lift more, that this small amount was all that she could carry, her response enraged the guard and she hit Betsie across her chest and neck with a belt. Corrie felt herself begin to move toward the guard in anger, but Betsie stopped her before anyone noticed and asked her to keep working. Corrie soon saw a red stain appear in Betsie's collar and noticed a lump beginning to swell on her neck. When she noticed Corrie looking at her wound, Betsie covered her neck and said, "Don't look at it, Corrie. Look at Jesus only."[3]

Despite her suffering, the love of Jesus sustained Betsie through her ordeal. Her health deteriorated until she was put in the prison hospital. One of the last things her sister told Corrie before her death was, "I pray every day that I will be allowed to [make a home for needy people, especially among their enemies, and care for them]. To show them that love is greater."[4] Betsie was sustained by the love of God, even in the midst of her suffering, and she was given the strength to love those who had hurt her.

Affirmations of God's love to us also help us experience healing from our pain and to overcome the terrible effects of rejection. Jesus tells us that he is the Good Shepherd who lays down his life for his sheep. He contrasts his care and love for us with that of a hired hand who runs away when he sees a wolf coming (John 10:11 – 13). In our "throwaway" culture, many people are not willing to stay committed to others when they sense trouble or difficulty — when they see a wolf coming. The result is disposable relationships and wounded hearts. Yet healing can come to those who have experienced the love of the Good Shepherd. In contrast to those "hired hands" who have disappointed us, he demonstrated his commitment to us by dying on our behalf.

GOD WILL TURN OUR PAIN INTO SOMETHING GOOD

In addition to knowing that God's love is greater than the evil in this world, there is a second great truth for us to remember, a truth that gives us strength to love those who hurt us: *God will turn our hurt and pain into something good.* Paul writes in Romans 8:28: "And we know that for those who love God all things work together for good." Not only is God's love greater than the wickedness and the evils committed by those who hurt us, but his power is also greater than their power. When we allow our emotions and our thoughts to be dominated and controlled by the wrongs that people have done to us, we give them an honor they do not deserve. We affirm that their influence on us is stronger than that of God. The good news that God can accomplish something greater — something good — despite the pain we are experiencing is an antidote to the injustice and hurt we feel.

The truth of God's sovereignty over the evil done to us is well illustrated in the story of Joseph and his brothers. Joseph's brothers were jealous of their brother, and they turned against him, selling him into slavery in Egypt. Over the years, God miraculously and sovereignly raised Joseph to become the second most powerful person in the land of Egypt. Subsequently he was reunited with his family. But after his father died, Joseph's brothers feared that he would use his power to take revenge on them (see Gen. 50:17–20). They "came and fell down before him and said, 'Behold, we are your servants.'" The Bible tells us that "Joseph wept when they spoke to him" — one of eight times recorded that Joseph wept.

Joseph had certainly experienced great pain, yet the love of God had softened his heart, moving him to cry when relating to his brothers. He told them not to worry: "Do not fear, for am I in the place of God? As for you, you meant evil against me, but God meant it for good, to bring it about that many people should be kept alive, as they are today." Though Joseph had suffered for many years because of the sin of his brothers' jealousy, he was able to look at his suffering with eyes of faith in God's sovereignty.

A friend of mine was once discipled by a mature Christian shortly after he became a believer in Christ. During their times of confession and prayer, my friend shared with this man a secret sin in his life, but he did not confess this to his wife. Subsequently, his mentor had an affair and ended up leaving his wife. When this man's wife came to him asking for help with the divorce proceedings, my friend faced a dilemma. He knew that her ex-husband could use his knowledge of his secret sin and could expose the secret. At the same time, my friend also knew that he had to do the right thing and help this woman in need.

Just as my friend had feared, his former mentor and discipler sent a letter to his wife, describing the sin he had kept hidden from her. She was devastated when she read the letter, but with confession, prayer, and some time to rebuild trust, God's grace won through and brought healing to their marriage. Afterward, my friend shared that he and his wife were now experiencing a level of freedom in their marriage that they had not had in many years. Previously, he had lived with the constant fear that his wife would find out his secret. Now that the sin had been exposed, that fear was gone, and there was great freedom and even deeper trust in their relationship. God can use the attacks of our enemies and the pain we suffer to accomplish something greater. He can turn every hurtful situation into something good for us.

Here, then, are two great truths we must meditate on and grasp deep in our hearts, truths that can help us to forgive people who hurt us. We begin by believing these two truths, even if we don't feel them. The Christian life is a life of faith, trusting that what God says is true and that it has power to save us and heal us. As we begin to believe that God's love for us is greater than the wickedness we face and that he will turn this situation into good, we find that it is not as difficult to forgive people who hurt us. When we struggle, we can ask God, who gives generously to those who ask him, to increase our faith and help us believe. When Jesus taught his disciples that they should forgive a brother who sins against them and repents, if necessary, up to seven times in a day, their response was to say to him, "Increase our faith!" (Luke 17:5).[5] When our hearts struggle with God's truth, we should ask for the same.

Sadly, not all Christians *want* to believe these truths. Many Christians want to cling tightly to an identity as a victim, believing that they have been wronged in a way that cannot be healed or forgiven. This gives them an excuse to nurture their anger and negative feelings about others. Self-pity is a reliable friend who gladly satisfies our innate desire to feel sorry for ourselves. Though our friends may tire of listening to our tale of woe, self-pity always provides us with a ready audience. One of the most difficult challenges I have had in my years of ministry is persuading people to apply God's love and sovereignty to their wounds. Believing the two powerful truths we have looked at inevitably forces us to part ways with our self-pity.

WE MUST ACT DECISIVELY

In his book *Total Forgiveness*, R. T. Kendall tells the story of a woman who had a car accident that caused her to live with constant neck pain for twenty-two years. She could not turn her head, not even to look in the mirror while driving, and so she had to forfeit her driving license. Margaret Moss, the wife of a London pastor, once asked her whether she had ever prayed for the driver who had caused her accident. "No," she replied. Knowing that the grace of God is often released through the power of forgiveness, Margaret suggested to this woman that she pray for the man who had hit her car. The woman prayed, saying the words "I forgive him" out loud. Then, Margaret asked her to verbally ask for God's blessing on the man. As she began to bless the man who had caused the accident, her pain began to leave her. By the next morning, she could move her neck freely for the first time in twenty-two years.[6]

Because the wrongs that people commit against us can have long and lasting effects on our lives, it is necessary for us to take decisive steps to experience the freedom that Christ offers to us. Those who have hurt us do not *deserve* to be forgiven. Often, they will not even accept that they have sinned against us. Yet even though they do not deserve forgiveness, we must learn to extend it to them, both for the sake of the gospel and for our own healing. When Jesus said that if we do not forgive others, our heavenly Father will not forgive us (Matt. 6:14–15), he was implying that *our failure to forgive blocks God's grace from coming into our lives.* In other words, the love of God comes in and goes out of the same door. If we close the door by refusing to extend God's love to others through forgiveness, we also close ourselves off from the grace of God entering our lives.

Lewis Smedes, in his book *Forgive and Forget*, says that by deciding to forgive, "you set a prisoner free, but you discover that the real prisoner was yourself."[7] We need to learn to forgive people, regardless of whether we can directly relate to them. *Christianity Today* recently published the account of Wess Stafford, president of Compassion International, detailing the abuse that he suffered as a child living at a boarding school for missionary kids in West Africa. The story also recorded how he was delivered from the pain of those terrible experiences.[8] Following the publication of his story, Wess wrote, "Ever since my story appeared in *Christianity Today*, the most common question I heard was, 'How did you move from pain to deliverance?' My replies to readers is a single word: *forgiveness.*"

Stafford says that at age 17, he realized that those who hurt him "would never apologize. They weren't even sorry. So I chose to forgive them anyway." He remembers saying, "Get out of my life.... What you did to me will not define me. You stole my childhood, but you cannot have the rest of my life. Get out—I forgive you." He gives this counsel to those who have suffered: "If you have never been able to forgive, you are allowing the person to live rent-free in your heart. It's costing him nothing and costing you everything. Perhaps it's time you evicted him through forgiveness."[9]

Christian patience does not condone the wrongs that are done. Genuine love does not sweep sin under a rug and pretend that nothing has happened. Instead, the power of patience in Christian love is shown by a refusal to hit back, despite the sin that is committed. This is a counter-cultural response—even in the church! We need Christians to cultivate intentionally an atmosphere where revenge is not tolerated, where we train ourselves to respond in light of the gospel of God's undeserved forgiveness, not as a response to our wounds or an instinct to protect ourselves.

⸝ ⸝ ⸝

Christian relationships today need to cultivate and practice a committed love—the kind of love Paul is describing in 1 Corinthians 13:4. More than ever before, the world needs to see this love in action, as Christians show patience and forgiveness to one another and point others to the radical love of God for those who have rejected him and his ways.

CHAPTER 5

PATIENCE ENCOUNTERING JUSTICE

1 CORINTHIANS 13:4A

"YOU JUST DON'T UNDERSTAND what I've been through."

"It's been ten years, and I am still suffering everyday from what he has done to me."

"You want me to forgive him, just like that? That's impossible!"

It is easy for us to say, "Love is patient," but as we saw in the last chapter, extending forgiveness to those who have wronged us is not so easy because it seems so unfair or unjust. "How can God ignore the wrong done to me? It's so unfair just to forgive someone." Perhaps you have heard sentiments like that. You may have even felt this way yourself at times.

God is just, and because he is just, all sin must be punished. Paul says, "Do not be deceived: God is not mocked, for whatever one sows, that will he also reap" (Gal. 6:7). Edward John Carnell refers to this as "the moral cycle," a cycle of actions and corresponding consequences that actively reveal the justice of God, a cycle that we do not have a right to personally complete.[1] Our sense of justice is a God-given instinct, a prompting we feel within us that says, "Sin *should* be punished." We must avoid simplistic understandings of the gospel that trumpet showing mercy at the *expense* of justice. The Bible teaches us clearly that when God saved sinful humanity, he did not ignore the serious breach of justice that sin represented. God did not overcome justice with love or ignore the demands of his justice. No, he *satisfied* justice through the loving sacrifice of his Son.

It can bring us some relief to know that all sin will indeed be punished. In his journals, John Wesley, after describing how a person had been illtreated, resulting in his premature death, wrote, "But still our comfort is, 'There is a God that judgeth in the earth.'"[2] When people ask the question, "How can he get away with such a crime?" we answer: "But he won't get away. He will have to face the awesome judgment of God one day." The doctrine of judgment is a powerful truth that can destroy the root of bitterness in our hearts, the sense that we are always a victim at the mercy of the sins of others.

Bitterness is often caused by a belief that the person who has hurt us will somehow escape from punishment. We wrongly assume that they have got away scot-free while we must live with the wounds they have inflicted. But the truth of God's judgment reminds us that no one gets away with sin. Sin is *always* punished. In the end, there are only two ways that sin is paid for: we pay it at the cost of our own blood, or Jesus pays it at the cost of his.

PATIENCE AND FORGIVENESS ACTIVATE LOVE

A key element in the biblical teaching on forgiveness and patience is that forgiveness is a means of God's healing. When we forgive people, we do not condone, excuse, or tolerate their sin. If we tried to avenge wrong according to the laws of justice, God knows we would make a mess of it! We are usually too emotionally involved in situations and too weak to be able to exercise good moral judgment. So God takes the matter of final, ultimate judgment out of our hands. He alone renders final judgment on our lives. Paul puts it this way: "Beloved, never avenge yourselves, but leave it to the wrath of God, for it is written, 'Vengeance is mine, I will repay, says the Lord'" (Rom. 12:19).

Yet there is something we can do, a way for us to respond when we are hurt. Paul goes on to say: "To the contrary, 'if your enemy is hungry, feed him; if he is thirsty, give him something to drink; for by so doing you will heap burning coals on his head'" (Rom. 12:20). Loving a person who has hurt us activates the love of God in a way that brings healing to our wounds and releases God's provision of strength. We follow in the footsteps of our Lord and exercise the most effective weapon against evil: good deeds motivated by love. As Paul says in the next verse: "Do not be overcome by evil, but overcome evil with good" (Rom 12:21).

Once, when the great Indian evangelist Sadhu Sundar Singh was preaching on the banks of a holy river, someone threw sand into his eyes. Several Hindu holy men who were present at the time were angered that a preacher had been treated this way, and they grabbed hold of the man to take him in to the police. Sundar Singh, after returning from washing the mud out of his eyes, saw what was happening and immediately went to plead on behalf of the man who had hurt him. He managed to secure his release and then returned to his preaching. The stunned man was so impressed that he not only begged Sundar Singh's forgiveness, he also became a seeker after the truth and accompanied him on his evangelistic journeys.[3]

How do our acts of love and kindness "overcome" evil? Why does love succeed where retaliation fails? Paul tells us in Romans 12 that the one who has caused the hurt will be so shocked by our response of love that when we love in this way, we "will heap burning coals on his head" (12:20). In other words, our love will negate the satisfaction that our enemy feels in hurting us and will "bring shame on wrongdoers so that they will repent of their evil."[4]

WHAT IF THEY REPENT?

Some will find satisfaction in knowing that God will judge sin, and this knowledge of God's judgment will calm their sense of moral outrage. But what if a person repents, as we saw in the example of Sundar Singh? Will you be disappointed and say to yourself, "Rats! No more punishment for him!"? It's not that simple. When a person genuinely repents of sin and turns from the evil he or she has committed, several things should happen. Each of these should bring a measure of healing to the person who has been wronged.

First, those who have committed a wrong may still have to live with the consequences of their actions. Sometimes those consequences are obvious, like a prison term. Other times, they are less obvious. King David committed adultery with Bathsheba, the wife of Uriah, and then sent Uriah to the frontlines in a battle and engineered a situation that resulted in his being killed. David repented and was forgiven by God, and Uriah's wife, Bathsheba, became David's wife and the mother of King Solomon. But the prophet Nathan warned David that there would still be consequences: "the sword shall never depart from your house" (2 Sam. 12:10). David's life following his sin is loaded with painful experiences within his family, especially with his children.

Second, if a person has genuinely repented, their life should, as John the Baptist said, "bear fruit in keeping with repentance" (Matt. 3:8). This would include evidence of genuine sorrow that is expressed to the hurt person, which can often go a long way toward healing his or her own wounds. If there is some way restitution can be made, that also should be done. For example, a person who stole funds should do everything he can to replace the funds he took.

Here is a common scenario I have seen many times. A husband nearly wrecks his home through an addiction to alcohol. His wife refuses to give up on him and prays for his conversion. Her prayers are answered: he gives up his drink and becomes a follower of Christ. His dramatic conversion makes him an instant celebrity in the church. He is invited all over to share his testimony and becomes active in ministry. Yet while he is enjoying his newfound celebrity status, his wife continues to struggle. She still has wounds that only the tender loving care and remorse of her husband can heal. He needs to continue working to bring healing to the wounds he has inflicted on his family. For this reason, we discourage those who "graduate" from our drug rehabilitation program from going public with their testimony immediately after they have experienced liberation from their addiction.

Third, and most important, we must remember that for this person to be forgiven, the spotless Son of God had to be punished through the most brutal form of execution—crucifixion. Christ's substitution on behalf of a sinner *more* than completes the moral cycle. On account of Christ, a hurt person can be assured that justice has been served. The price for the sin committed has been fully paid by the suffering and death of the Son of God.

A FEW MORE PRACTICAL ACTIONS

As evidenced at the cross, love is more than an inspiring idea—it is always expressed in concrete ways. So let me suggest several additional *practical* things to consider when extending God's radical love in forgiveness toward repentant sinners. These suggestions will help to ensure that our love for others does not minimize the serious affront of sin to the holiness of God.

EXERCISING CHURCH DISCIPLINE

Forgiving someone is not the end of the process—it is really just the beginning. Radical love includes a responsibility to help a person overcome the weakness that caused him or her to hurt someone in the first place. Hebrews 12:6 says, "For the Lord disciplines the one he loves, and chastises every son whom he receives." Isaiah adds, "If favor is shown to the wicked, he does not learn righteousness" (Isa. 26:10). Loving discipline brings with it the pain of deprivation. Continuing to do favors for a person who continues in sin is not loving; it may actually harm the person.

It may be best for the person who has been hurt to hand over the discipline process to another person, a neutral third party. In the church, consultation among trusted leaders is the way of wisdom for most disciplinary situations. Disciplining people is not an occasion for hasty, impulsive decisions. It is always a painful and complicated process, with room for misunderstanding on all sides. Discipline that follows a biblical model and seeks the restoration of the wrongdoer (1 Cor. 5:5; 1 Tim. 1:20) can be extremely draining on the leadership of an organization or church. It requires a commitment to love and care for the wrongdoer that, sadly, is not all that common today. Radical love requires a willingness to pay the price and commit to the painful process of discipline. That is an important aspect of Christian patience.

It is much easier to ignore the problem or to encourage a person to leave a group and go elsewhere for fellowship. Sometimes a wrongdoer will leave the church or refuse to participate in a process of restoration. Instead of being glad that they have left, we should be saddened by this, knowing that when people leave the community to which they belonged when they fell into sin, they leave behind their best hope for genuine healing. The best place for a wrongdoer to be healed is the same family in which they were when they did wrong.

CONFRONTING THE PERSON WHO HURT US

We should be prepared to confront sin in others and make it clear when we have been wronged by them. Sometimes hurt people are advised to forgive those who have hurt them without ever talking to that person. I have seen this happen most commonly with a wife who is told that she should forgive her unkind husband, yet she never confronts him about his sinful behavior. Some will even praise her for her long-suffering fortitude and enduring patience. I have seen wives who have done this for many years begin to show signs of severe depression in their older years. As they grow older and no longer have the capacity to hide their feelings, the pain that had been there all along, carefully hidden and controlled, finally surfaces.

Matthew 18:15–20 outlines a procedure for us to follow when a brother or sister sins against us. We are first to talk to them alone. If that does not work, we should take one or two other witnesses along. If that does not work, we are to tell it to the church, which will act on behalf of the offended party through its leaders. If all of this fails to elicit a response of repentance, the person is to be treated "as a Gentile and a tax collector." This suggests that the person is to be expelled from the church community and should be treated like an unbeliever. Of course, this does not mean that we no longer care for this person's restoration. We should keep in mind that Jesus' ministry was marked by his loving, friendly care for tax collectors and those who were not welcome in the religious community.

Sometimes, it is impossible to confront the person who has hurt us. I have found that in some of the more serious cases, where deep wounds have been inflicted by a person who is no longer accessible or alive, it may helpful to use symbolic acts as a substitute for direct confrontation. I have encouraged sexually, physically, or verbally abused persons to write letters to the offending party, letters that are never actually delivered to the people who abused or hurt them. Instead, we have the letters read aloud in my presence (possibly along with my wife). We then follow these readings with pronouncements of Scripture that depict the cleansing of the wounded person. Afterward, we usually burn the letter as a symbol of their hurt being removed.

The ideal, in every case, is reconciliation with the wrongdoer, as Jesus stated (cf. Matt. 18:15). But there will never be true reconciliation until a person accepts that he or she has done something wrong. John, in one of his letters to the church, describes something he calls "walking in the light." This is an experience of unity, rooted in integrity, that involves confession of sin and acceptance that we have sinned against others. He concludes by saying, "But if we walk in the light, as he is in the light, we have fellowship with one another" (1 John 1:7). It is possible to maintain superficial friendships with people who refuse to accept their wrongdoing. But true fellowship and reconciliation will require a person to take responsibility for his or her actions.

LEGAL ACTION

Sometimes when a civil offense or a criminal act is committed—like robbery, encroachment, rape, and sexual abuse—it is necessary to hand the situation over to the legal authorities. In some situations, a failure to report such crimes could result in legal liability. It is necessary to restrain a rapist or a sexual abuser to prevent that person from continuing to commit this crime.

When the Old Testament speaks of the law of retaliation (*lex talionis*), demanding "life for life, eye for eye, tooth for tooth, hand for hand, foot for foot" (Deut. 19:21), it is not talking about taking revenge. It is presenting the laws of the land. That is how crime should be dealt within that legal system. Paul validated this and applied it to legal systems outside the Jewish people of God to whom it was originally given. He says that a "secular" government authority "is the servant of God, an avenger who carries out God's wrath on the wrongdoer" (Rom. 13:4b).

That said, not all civil offenses will need to be reported. In some cases, it is possible to ignore minor offenses. For example, if a neighbor has a party that goes on until late at night and their noise disturbs you, you may decide to ignore it and not report them to the authorities because it is a rare occurrence.

IMMEDIATE DANGER

There are times when the most loving act we can take involves immediate, decisive action to protect someone from harm. For example, if I see a person coming with a knife to stab a friend, the most appropriate action is not to tell the person they are forgiven or to tell them, "God bless you, I will pray for you!" The best thing to do is tackle them to the ground. Violent people cannot be reasoned with when they are in the passion of the moment. They must be restrained through appropriate means. Restraining a compulsive gambler or someone who is chemically dependent may require securing a legal ruling that restricts that person's use of his or her bank account.

AGITATING FOR JUSTICE

When people are being exploited by an employer or a government institution, it may be necessary to institute a form of nonviolent resistance to the injustice—like a procession, a picket campaign, or a strike. The Methodists were influential in the start of labor unions in Britain. Japan's first trade union was founded by Toyohiko Kagawa (1888–1960), who was both a social activist and an evangelist. Sadly, in recent years some labor unions have abused their influence and taken steps that hurt productivity. Yet despite these negatives, we must continue to recognize that employers who continue to exploit their workers unjustly need to be confronted using appropriate means.

, , ,

In each of the situations we have considered, exercising love requires practical action that is willing to confront sin directly and challenge it. Yet as we confront evil, our response should be informed by the gospel and driven by a long-term desire to see a person experience the healing power of God's grace. When I was in elementary school, children often kept autograph books with signatures and comments from their friends. I still remember what one teacher wrote in my book: "Retaliate like an oyster which, when hurt, yields a pearl."

When Christians respond to hatred, they respond with love. Throughout history, Christians have been known as people who love their enemies and turn the other cheek when slapped (Matt. 5:39). As those who have known the patience of God in dealing with our own weaknesses and sins, we are more than willing to forgive offenses and exercise patience with those who have wronged us.

CHAPTER 6

CONCERN IN ACTION

1 CORINTHIANS 13:4B

A FRIEND OF the British Methodist preacher William Sangster once said, "Whenever [Sangster] met a person, his attitude seemed to be, 'How can I help this person.'" When Sangster died, his wife received nearly 1,400 letters from people, and more than a thousand of them mentioned some specific help that Sangster had given to that person.[1] After spending three chapters on patience as the first characteristic of love, we now move to Paul's second characteristic: "Love is ... kind" (1 Cor. 13:4). Christians are people who are kind; they are actively concerned for the welfare of others.

In the second century, Christians were called *Christiani*, meaning "Christ people." The African church father Tertullian (c. 160–225) tells us that after observing the way Christians lived and seeing how they treated others, they so affected their pagan neighbors that they were given a slightly different name. Instead of calling them *Christiani*, the pagan people began referring to them as *chrestiani*, or people "made up of mildness or kindness."[2] If Christians are those who seek to "make love [their] aim" in life (1 Cor. 14:1 RSV), then showing kindness to others is a key part of fulfilling this ambition. Though all religions teach people to be kind, the distinctly Christian feature of kindness, as we have seen with forgiveness, is that it is a *response to the kindness bestowed on us by God*. As Paul said, "Be kind to one another, tenderhearted, forgiving one another, as God in Christ forgave you" (Eph. 4:32).

KINDNESS AND HAPPINESS

Kindness can make a home a happy place to live. If a husband makes love his aim, being kind to his wife becomes one of his primary ambitions, as his most important relationship on earth is with his wife. His wife in turn sees her husband continue to show kindness to her, often at some personal cost, which brings her great joy. The result is a happy home — and happiness is the greatest wealth a home can have.

My favorite book on the Christian idea of being a servant to others is a book called *Slave of Christ*,[3] written by the renowned New Testament scholar Murray Harris. Harris shows how servanthood or slavery is a metaphor used in the New Testament to describe total and complete commitment to a person … or to Christ. This idea of being committed to someone was more than an academic concept for Dr. Harris. Several years ago, Dr. Harris's wife was stricken with multiple sclerosis, making it necessary for him to take an early retirement from Trinity Evangelical Divinity School in Chicago and return to his homeland of New Zealand. Doctors had advised him that given his wife's condition, returning home was the best option for her long-term care. After returning to New Zealand, his wife's situation progressively got worse and she eventually had to be cared for full-time.

Writing to me in September 2010 about his wife's condition, Dr. Harris made it clear to me that he felt he was "privileged to be a full-time caregiver." His wife, Jennifer, saddened that he was sacrificing so much to care for her, once told him, "I wish you could get on with your *own work*!" To this Harris replied to her, "Caring for you *is* my work; anything else is extra."

Kindness leads to genuine joy in relationships. As I write this book, my own wife is battling cancer (which we hope is not terminal). This past Christmas was unusual for me because I did little preaching. Unlike the thirty-four years of Christmases prior, I spent most of my time at home with my wife. I honestly think it was one of my happiest Christmases ever. When love is activated and our acts of service are motivated by kindness toward others, an inevitable consequence is joy.

KINDNESS IN SITUATIONS OF CONFLICT

John Chrysostom (c. 347–407) was the bishop of Constantinople, and he is commonly regarded as the greatest Bible expositor of the early church. Chrysostom (meaning "golden-mouthed") was a nickname his contemporaries gave him because of the "beauty of his preaching."[4] In his meditations on 1 Corinthians 13 Chrysostom says that we must show kindness to others "in order to appease and extinguish that fire [of anger]." When we are kind, we "soothe and comfort ... and by so doing, we cure the sore and heal the wound of passion."[5] With the love that God gives us, we look for opportunities to show kindness to the opposite party. We pounce on opportunities when we see needs we can help meet.

Kindness is a form of concern in action toward *all* types of people in *all* sorts of circumstances. Like patience, kindness can be extended to those who have harmed us, and in this way it can be an agent of peace in times of conflict. Many Christians around the world attend church in an area where there is armed conflict or persecution. Even if you do not live in an area like this, it is common to experience conflict in your place of work or school. Nor are Christian organizations exempt from this. In fact, the pain of relational conflict can be worse in a church or a Christian organization because we tend to expect more from our fellow Christians and are disappointed when such conflicts develop. Showing kindness to those with whom we are in conflict can be one of the greatest agents of healing.

In a previous chapter I mentioned a young man from the minority Tamil race in Sri Lanka who lived in my home for six months after his house had been burned down by a mob of people from the Sinhala race (my race). He often tells me that it was impossible for him to give in to hatred for the Sinhala race because he had experienced such love from other Sinhala people. He has now devoted his life to academic studies on how to solve ethnic conflicts similar to the one he has experienced.

I have a colleague named Jeyaraj, who was arrested on suspicion of being a terrorist and sent to a prison for people convicted or suspected of involvement in terrorism. He was kept there for fifteen months without any charges being made against him. During the time of the war in our country, this was an all-too-common occurrence. This particular incident was his fourteenth arrest! After an initial few days of hurt, however, Jeyaraj got together with another Christian there and began an amazing ministry in the prison, which resulted in many people coming to Christ.

Jeyaraj is a minority Tamil, and since he had been unjustly arrested and kept in prison by the Sinhala establishment, it would not have surprised anyone if he harbored some deep resentment against the Sinhalese people. Sometime after his release from prison, Jeyaraj needed to spend some time in the hospital because of various internal injuries related to the abuse he had endured during his numerous arrests. Another colleague called me to let me know that there was a welfare officer from the prison who was spending a lot of time with Jeyaraj, so much so that he was not able to have time alone with his wife.

When I visited Jeyaraj in hospital, the welfare officer was there. When I arrived, he left the room to have a cup of tea in the cafeteria, and I asked Jeyaraj why this officer was spending so much time with him. He let me know that they had, in fact, become good friends in prison. At various times when the officer was depressed or discouraged, Jeyaraj had offered comfort and counsel to him. After hearing that Jeyaraj was in the hospital, the officer had taken leave and made the three-hour journey to spend time with him. What made this all the more amazing was that the officer was Sinhalese. A young man, held unjustly in prison, was now ministering God's kindness to the very prison official he should have hated!

That is evidence of radical love in action.

SOME CAUTIONS

There are countless stories of people who have tried to extend kindness to others and have been hurt in return. The fact that we bear a cross reminds us that our attempts to show kindness to others do not render us immune from misunderstanding and pain. Yet there are things we can do to exercise caution when extending kindness to our enemies and those in need of help. These cautions can reduce or minimize the impact that others can have on us, particularly if it is negative.

WE ARE NOT MESSIAHS

The first caution we must keep in mind, as we serve others in kindness, is that we do not have to meet every need we encounter. A need does not automatically indicate a call from God to meet it. We are human, and there are limitations to what we can do. Leaders should see that a structure is set in place to ensure that the needs of all the people in their group are addressed, but they do not have to do all the work themselves. Their role is often to facilitate a connection between the needy and those who can help them. We may direct some needy people to others who can help them, and we may direct some helpers to people who have needs.

We must be especially careful when helping people of the opposite sex. Sometimes what starts as a harmless and beautiful partnership within the body of Christ can become an emotionally binding relationship.

Because it starts out beautifully and the slide into unhealthy intimacy takes place gradually, we may not even realize when a relationship has become unhealthy. Others who observe us or are aware of the relationship may sense this, and it is important that they are faithful to warn the people concerned. When such warnings are given, they must be heeded with utmost seriousness. A sure sign of danger on the horizon is when people refuse the warnings of the wise, as the book of Proverbs says many times.

THE PRIMARY PLACE TO SHOW LOVE IS THE HOME.

Sadly, I have often had family members of a Christian leader or a person in a helping profession tell me something like this: "He cares for everyone except his family. When he comes home he is too tired to think about us." However busy we may be helping others, our primary responsibility is always the care of our own families. This "balanced life" may be our cross to bear at times, because it requires us to do so many things and negotiate shifting priorities in different seasons of life and ministry.

Some people see the idea of the balanced life as an attempt to do everything in moderation. But this is not a biblical idea. Instead, it is more accurate to describe a balanced life as *obedience* in every area of life. But this is far from easy. The particular details of our obedience may change from week to week and from day to day. Still, we are attempting to do what we believe is God's will for us in this situation, knowing that he will help us to do it. Sometimes we must simply use our best judgment, trusting that the Lord will help us keep our commitments. At other times, we must say no to certain obligations in order to say yes to others.

I think of a father who serves as volunteer leader in his church. His son is running in a track meet and has made it to the finals. The race is at 3:00 p.m. on Saturday. But the father also has a meeting at 1:30 p.m. at church. He explains the situation to his son and tells him that he will try to be there for the finals. On Saturday, though he attends the church meeting, when the time comes for his son's track meet he excuses himself from the meeting and rushes to the field where the meet is being held. He parks his car, runs to the field, and gets there just before the son starts running. As he is running, the son hears his father voice urging him on. He is encouraged and, with a burst of speed, wins the race.

The father catches up with his son to congratulate him. The son notices that his father is panting, and he tells him, "I am the one who ran the race; why are you panting?" The father replies, "I needed to be here in time for your race, so I ran." In this case, the son is probably not going to be angry about his father's involvement in church. He knows that though his father cares for others in church, he is willing to pay the price of caring for him when necessary. I have found that fulfilling all my family obligations along with my ministry responsibilities can be tiring. But I have decided to take that tiredness on gladly, viewing it as the cross Christ would have me bear as I seek to be obedient to him in all areas of life.

BE PREPARED TO BE HURT

Not everyone we help responds positively to the help we offer them. Some will exploit us and try to get more from us than what is reasonable. Some will turn against us when we do something they do not like or we refuse one of their requests. Sometimes people may begin to move away from God, and the first person they blame is often the one who has sacrificially helped them in their walk with God. In times like this, we must act with love and hope, doing all we can to restore the relationship and to make it easy for the persons to return back to us and restore their relationship with God.

As Christians we are called to help hurting people. Yet as the title of a recent book puts it: *Hurt People Hurt People*.[6] There are people who are so broken and hurt that they retaliate against those who try to help them. Or you may try to help a person who hurts others, and those who have been hurt by this person are angry with you because you help him and speak up for him. Kindness can be costly, in many different ways.

DON'T BE BITTER ABOUT INGRATITUDE

You may find that you show kindness to someone, and then suddenly you do something he or she does not like. You refuse a request, speak out against a wrongful action, or point out something that needs to change in her life or refuse to take her side in a conflict. In response, all the help you have given to this person is forgotten. You are attacked or abandoned. When you are helping others, you must prepare yourself for the response of ingratitude. Ingratitude hurts. I imagine that Jesus must have been saddened to see that only one of the ten lepers he healed returned to thank him (Luke 17:12–19). But while such ingratitude can hurt, we should not let it ruin our lives or consume our thoughts. After all, should we expect any better treatment than Jesus received?

We must fight against letting ingratitude destroy our joy. We must severely resist any temptation to retaliate and hurt an ungrateful person.

The key to our resistance is remembering who and why we serve. If what we do is done for God, for his glory, and in response to his love for us, we can rest assured, secure in knowing that his love is sufficient for us, that he sees what we do so that we no longer crave praise from people. The Lord supplies all our needs.

People often get angry with their leaders when they are disciplined for some wrongdoing. Discipline is actually an act of kindness aimed at helping the persons overcome the weaknesses that caused them to sin. They may leave us angrily, join another group, and speak ill of us. Sometimes these other groups will use them in service, ignoring our disciplinary act of restricting their ministry. Yet when those people who left us face a serious problem, often they come back to us. They know we are principled people and that we can be trusted to give them genuine help. Such principled behavior brings a unique security to the group. In their time of trouble these people realize that we are consistent people. This may make these people want the security of being under our cover.

So let us keep loving people consistently, even after they have rebelled against our discipline. Such consistent love will help create an atmosphere where people trust others within the Christian community.

BEWARE OF CREATING DEPENDENCY

While it is good for us to be kind to people, we must always work toward weaning those who can manage on their own away from needing our help. As the saying goes, "Give a man a fish and you feed him for a day. Teach a man to fish and you feed him for a lifetime." Some people will require help over long periods of time, such as those with a handicap or the elderly. Others will need help overcoming a habit or changing an aspect of their lifestyle, and in these cases we help them most by eventually weaning them from needing further help.

In the ministry I do among the poor youth of Sri Lanka, we focus much of our attention on providing education to the children. We know that if these young people are equipped and taught to do well educationally, they have a better chance of breaking away from the cycle of generational poverty they are currently trapped in.

GET YOUR STRENGTH AND PRIMARY FULFILLMENT FROM GOD

A life of service to others can be draining, and there are often tiring and painful experiences. We must be strong to engage in this kind of service.

What better way is there to grow in strength than to spend time with God? Not only must we get our strength from God, but we must also get our primary fulfillment and identity from him. If we get too much fulfillment from our service, we may not be willing to hand it over to others. We may discover that we have come to enjoy the dependence that others have on us so much that we begin unconsciously to keep them dependent on us. When people fail and disappointments and criticism come, we will almost certainly be discouraged and angry; but if we get too much fulfillment from our work, discouragement and anger could become so severe that it cripples us and makes us ineffective. Our joy has been too dependent on the service we do and not on the Lord.

The one thing that we cannot do without is God's presence. How wonderful it is to know that he is always there and that he will never disappoint us. Deepening our friendship with God must always be our greatest aspiration in life. We must come to God daily to get our strength from him. I often tell our young staff at Youth for Christ that in the type of work we do, we should plan on entering into the world and getting bashed. Then, we return to God and he recharges our batteries. On the strength of that recharging, we go out again, ready to get bashed yet again. But we can always come back to God and find strength. He is an inexhaustible reservoir of healing for our souls. Finding strength and fulfillment from God is what enables us to engage in a lifetime of service.

, , ,

All these cautions should not discourage us from the wonderful call to love people by showing kindness to them. There is a story about the apostle John that is attributed to the Bible translator Jerome (c.345-c.419).[7] When John was extremely old and unable to walk, it is said that he had to be carried to attend church. Instead of giving a long talk for the sermon, he would only say a few words: "Little children, love one another, love one another, love one another." His disciples were beginning to grow weary of hearing this one line repeated over and over again, but he responded to them by saying that if they really loved one another, it would be enough, for it was the Lord's command.[8]

For a Christian, showing kindness to others is one of the highest priorities in life. But it can be costly as well. In the next chapter, we'll look at the question: *Is it worth showing kindness?* The answer, of course, is yes. But the reasons why may surprise you.

CHAPTER 7

IS IT WORTH SHOWING KINDNESS?

1 CORINTHIANS 13:4B

KINDNESS IS EASY to receive, but it is hard to practice. We can all agree that kindness is a wonderful thing, but not all are committed to actively living out a life of kindness. Why? Because kindness is costly. Showing kindness to others can get in the way of our plans. That is why it is necessary for us to understand *why* it is worthwhile to be kind.

WE ARE MADE IN THE IMAGE OF GOD

One of the most popular commands to love others in the Scriptures occurs in 1 John 4:7: "Beloved, let us love one another, for love is from God, and whoever loves has been born of God and knows God." John immediately follows up this way: "Anyone who does not love does not know God, because God *is* love" (4:8). Because God *is* love, and we are made in the image of God, loving others gives full expression to our humanity. A lack of love makes us subhuman.

Some people say that they can't be bothered with showing kindness to others because they must look after their own personal concerns. They wrongly assume that if they are able to achieve their dreams and satisfy their personal ambition, they will be happy. In truth, however, they will not. Selfishness is always unfulfilling because it denies an essential aspect of our humanity—the ability to love.

There are times when I am busy with a number of projects, and I suddenly learn that someone from Youth for Christ or our church family is ill in the hospital. At first, I'm not inclined to visit them because I am so loaded down with work. But I know I have no choice, so I reluctantly make the trip to the hospital. In all my years of ministry, I have never made a trip to visit someone in need without coming back happy that I made the trip. Despite what it does to my schedule, these unexpected opportunities to show kindness to people affirm my identity as a human being and as a child of God. Though it wasn't what I felt like doing, loving someone by showing them kindness has brought a great sense of fulfillment to my life.

Early in our ministry we welcomed a husband and wife, who had recently come to Christ and had been earning their living as carnival singers, into our home. Though it wasn't part of the original plan, this couple ended up living in a section of our home for almost seventeen years! The husband John would often get drunk and was addicted to gambling before his conversion. His sister, a woman named Indramony, was a devout Buddhist. But she was so impressed after seeing the change in her brother's life that she, too, was attracted to Christ. She was prone to nervous breakdowns and also came to stay in our home whenever she felt close to a breakdown. Eventually she, too, became a Christian. Her nervousness made her trust in God with greater consistency and urgency than some of us. This made Indramony into a prayer warrior.

For our part, we tried to ensure that she was not put under undue emotional strain and that she took her medicines regularly. She became a conduit of God's love through a vibrant intercessory prayer life. As she came to understand the gospel more fully, she was freed from her oppressive anxiety. Indramony lived for about twenty-five years after coming to Christ and died at the age of sixty after being hit by a bus while walking to church. She was a single woman with limited financial means, and so we were surprised when a large crowd attended her funeral. It was then that we realized just what an impact her kindness had made on many different people. We saw the fruit of a life spent in serving others through simple acts of kindness.

Indramony had spent her days caring for, visiting, and praying for those who were sick, lonely, elderly, and in any sort of need. When our children were small and my wife and I went on a long trip, she would come and stay with the children. Here is a person who would normally have been incapacitated as a result of her anxiety. She would have likely spent her days, apart from the transforming work of Christ, heavily drugged and confined to her house. But through the power of the gospel and the work of the Holy Spirit, she became a valiant servant of Christ. The love of Christ made her a *whole* person, and she found fulfillment in being an agent of Christ's love to others.

I often see the fruitfulness of Christlike kindness when I observe Christians who are advanced in years. My mother is now eighty-seven years old and blind. Parkinson's disease has left her unable to walk. By God's grace, she is not only a physical mother to her five children, but she is also our spiritual mother. Converted to Christ from Buddhism in her youth, my mother has walked with God for over seventy years now, and she radiates the love of Christ despite her physical affliction. When you meet her, her conversation is always about *other* people, about their needs and their welfare. When I visit her, I share updates and news with her, and it can be either good or bad. I find that in the middle of our conversation, she has slipped into prayer, speaking to God about the news I have shared with her. She has had many painful experiences in her life, and she has learned to forgive those who have hurt her. Seventy years of living and resting in the love of Christ have borne fruits that sustain her under extreme conditions of disability.

When I consider my mother, I notice what a contrast she is to other elderly people I know. I visit them and they are always complaining. They talk about their aches and their pains. They talk about how their children do not care for them. They may believe in Christ, but they do not seem to have the love of Christ. I observe little joy in their hearts, certainly nothing that is evident in the midst of their pain. Some people are like this because they have been badly wounded by others in their younger years. They remained polite and pleasant as long as they have control of their emotions. But as they grow older and lose control, depression sets in as the pain they were carrying begins to surface. O that someone would help them to experience God's healing grace!

Others are unhappy in their older years because they lived selfishly during their younger years. Because they did not take the time to cultivate meaningful friendships with others when they had time and energy to invest in others, they now lack the treasure of friendships, people who will stay close to them in their time of need. A life of selfishness has borne the bitter fruits of loneliness and unhappiness.

THE LOVE OF CHRIST CONTROLS US

The compulsion to love others should increase after one comes to Christ, the one who demonstrated his love to us by dying for us while we were still sinners (Rom. 5:8) and who fills us with his love (5:5). As the apostle John says, "We love because he first loved us" (1 John 4:19).

In 2 Corinthians 5 Paul explains why "a life of self-pleasing" was impossible for him to live,[1] for "the love of Christ controls us" (2 Cor. 5:14). The word "controls" can communicate two ideas. On the one hand, it can mean compulsion, in which case Paul is suggesting that love somehow pushes us or motivates us to action on behalf of others. On the other hand, control can mean a form of restraint, in which case it suggests the idea that love somehow restrains us from being selfish. Murray Harris (whose care for his ailing wife we described in the previous chapter) believes that both ideas are included in this verse. He writes: "Christ's love is a compulsive force in the life of believers, a dominating power that effectively eradicates choice in that it leaves them no option but to live for God ... and Christ."[2]

I have encountered devout Christians who had once been active in Christian service but then suffered a deep disappointment or a setback, such as the inexplicable breakup of a love relationship. In their pain they say something like this to themselves, "I have served others long enough, and now I must look after myself." They drop out of Christian service, sometimes even leaving the church. Yes, there can be value in refraining from active service after a particularly traumatic or disappointing experience to take time to heal and restore your emotional strength. But at some point, the path to health and healing leads a follower of Christ to return to serving others. Thankfully, most of the people I have met who have been stuck in this place of weakness have eventually come back. I say thankfully, because I know that if they do not make this return, they are condemning themselves to a life that lacks happiness, a life that is not fulfilling.

When we are in fellowship with God, his love enters us and remains in us. When we show kindness to others, his love is revealed through us. Love, in this sense, benefits both the recipient and the one who gives it. It is what enables us to become happy people. Prayer is a great example of this. Describing the prospect of his release from prison, Paul tells the Philippian Christians, "I know that through your prayers and the help of the Spirit of Jesus Christ this will turn out for my deliverance" (Phil. 1:19). It is almost as if Paul is putting the prayers of the Philippians on par with the help of the Holy Spirit as one of the things that gives him hope for his release. Praying, then, is a powerful act of kindness to another.

When we show kindness to others by praying for them, we are also in intimate touch with God, who is the source of love. This dynamic relationship with God through prayer opens up our lives for intimacy with God, which also means our lives are opened up for an inrush of God's love. Thus, love is coming in from God through vital contact with him and going out from us as we pray for others. This interplay of love going out and coming in is a refreshing exercise. Our love life is fully operational. Soon we begin to glow with the joy that comes from God's love filling our lives.

A year ago I was able to reduce my executive responsibilities in Youth for Christ after serving thirty-five years as its director, though I am still on staff as a mentor, teacher, and counselor. Though I am not yet retired, I spend more time at home now. Since I do not need to leave home early on most mornings, I am able to linger in God's presence praying for people more than before. This has been one of the most beautiful aspects of my new job. Don't wait until you are retired to spend time praying, though. There is no guarantee that you are going to be willing to make time for prayer after retirement if you lose the taste for prayer before your retirement!

LOVE IS THE COMMAND OF GOD

Loving our neighbors is one of the most important behaviors for a Christian. It is something we are commanded to do. Consider a sample of references from the teaching of Jesus:

- "And if anyone forces you to go one mile, go with him two miles. Give to the one who begs from you, and do not refuse the one who would borrow from you.... Love your enemies and pray for those who persecute you" (Matt. 5:41–42, 44).
- "And whoever gives one of these little ones even a cup of cold water because he is a disciple, truly, I say to you, he will by no means lose his reward" (Matt. 10:42).
- "You shall love your neighbor as yourself" (Matt. 19:19). This command is repeated eight times in the New Testament.[3] Luke illustrates this command by the parable of the good Samaritan, who cared for the wounded traveler (Luke 10:30–35).

The fact that God has commanded us to be kind to people is itself a sufficient reason to do it. We know that God will never ask us to do something that is ultimately hurtful. There are times when kindness may feel costly, but often the very things that are most costly to us God can transform into a means of blessing. Is this not what Jesus taught when he said, "Whoever would save his life will lose it, but whoever loses his life for my sake will find it" (Matt. 16:25)?

Several times, I have had the opportunity to speak at the Urbana Missionary Conference for students in the United States. In 1990, I was scheduled to speak there, and I was planning to fly to Chicago for the conference on the evening of Christmas Day. I had been busy in the days preceding the trip, and so I was worried that jet lag and tiredness would adversely affect my speaking. On Christmas Eve, the night before I was to leave for my trip to the United States, I went to bed around 2.00 a.m. I had been up late preparing my sermon for the Christmas service at our church. It felt as if I had slept for only a few minutes when I suddenly heard a loud knock at our door. Our neighbors did not have electricity in their home, and they had a child who was very, very sick with a stomach ailment. In the darkness, they had mistakenly given him skin lotion instead of medicine for the stomach, so I immediately got dressed and rushed them to the hospital. They were poor and I was concerned they would not get good treatment, so I stayed with them until morning to ensure they got what they needed for their child.

I came home from the hospital that morning and went straight to church to preach. I was hoping to have a good sleep after our afternoon Christmas meal, but yet again, I slept no more than a few minutes when I was woken up by someone who had come to see me. I visited with that person for awhile and then went back to sleep after he left.

Once again, a few minutes passed and there was another visitor. I realized that the afternoon of Christmas Day was not a good time to sleep! Eventually, I gave up and played some games with my children. But I knew that I still needed sleep. That night, I boarded a direct flight from Colombo to Amsterdam en route to Chicago. We had about 50 passengers on a 350 seat plane, and I had four seats all to myself. I used the extra seats to make a comfortable bed and slept the longest I have ever slept on a flight in my many years of traveling ministry. It was an exciting blessing for me to know that when God had sent those needy persons to my house earlier that day, he had known that I was going to get the sleep I needed the next night! I was reminded of Paul's words to the Thessalonian Church: "He who calls you is faithful; he will surely do it" (1 Thess 5:24).

HOW THE WORLD WILL KNOW

As ideas and practices that are at odds with the Christian faith began to rise in popularity in the 1970s and 80s, several evangelical voices spoke out. One of the loudest and most articulate voices was Francis Schaeffer (1912–1984). Schaeffer was best known as an apologist and an evangelist to intellectual seekers after truth. Yet Schaeffer's apologetics were about more than convincing the mind. He argued that it was wrong to separate apologetics from a life of love and once famously described the love and kindness shown by Christians as "the final apologetic."[4] In recent years, a book summarizing his apologetic approach has been published, entitled *Truth with Love.*[5] It describes how Schaeffer showed kindness to individuals, often at tremendous personal cost, and how his kindness toward them was a key influence leading them to respond positively to the gospel.

Jesus says to us, "Let your light shine before others, so that they may see your good works and give glory to your Father who is in heaven" (Matt. 5:16). The truth is that most non-Christians are not all that interested in hearing the message of the gospel. People lead busy lives, and they have their own ambitions and dreams. They are often satisfied, on the surface, with what the world offers to them. So it takes something to surprise them or to make them *want* to listen. I find that many are attracted by the prospect of experiencing God's power to heal or are looking for him to meet some other need in their life. This is nothing new; it was true in the early church as well. The miracles of the apostles attracted attention, drawing people to hear the message. But what we often miss is that in addition to the miraculous, the love of ordinary Christians, with a willingness to serve those in need, often attracted the attention of unbelievers around them.

You may have read that Christianity became the religion of the Roman Empire in the fourth century through the edict of the emperor Constantine. In reality, however, a combination of factors led to the spread of Christianity across cultures. Sociologist Rodney Stark has written a helpful book, *The Rise of Christianity*, in which he looks at how Christianity spread throughout the world. As the subtitle puts it, his book demonstrates *How the Obscure, Marginal Jesus Movement Became the Dominant Religious Force in the Western World in a Few Centuries.*

Stark presents several key factors that led to this mass movement of the population toward accepting the teachings of Christ. He demonstrates how two great epidemics affected large portions of the population during those first centuries. If people affected by the disease were cared for properly, there was a good chance they would survive the plague. Unfortunately, because people feared the disease, when a member of their family would contract it, the other members often left the house and abandoned the sick person. But the Christians did not leave. The willingness of Christians to stay and show kindness toward their sick family members, caring for them in their time of need, naturally led to a rise in the number of Christians who survived.

In addition to caring for their own, many Christians also chose to care for those left behind by their non-Christian family members. Christians caring for the sick was one of the main factors that contributed to the conversion of large numbers of people in the Roman Empire.[6]

Today, many evangelicals are branded as arrogant and unkind because of their convictions. Christian beliefs about sexuality and the uniqueness of Christ run counter to the popular consensus. Though people may reject the truth and feel enmity toward what we believe, we must not forget the teaching of Jesus about our enemies: "You have heard that it was said, 'You shall love your neighbor and hate your enemy.' But I say to you, Love your enemies and pray for those who persecute you" (Matt. 5:43–44). I am convinced that servanthood is one of the best ways to answer the objections people have to our unique beliefs. They may dislike what we believe, but they cannot help but be impressed by the way we live.

LOVE BRINGS ETERNAL REWARDS

Many years ago, Garry Trudeau in his cartoon strip Doonesbury made the comment, "We live in a world where people prefer to be envied than to be esteemed."[7] I believe his statement gets at an important distinction, one we often miss. We tend to *envy* people for their success, which is typically judged according to earthly values. But we *esteem* people for their character.

Godly character is the fruit of a transformed heart, and God is the best judge of the motives that lead people to act the way they do. In the world, it is all too easy to miss the sacrificial service of those who follow God's agenda. It is rarely visible, and some who labor for many years in sacrificial service to others can be tempted to grow bitter if their efforts are never seen or recognized. But knowing that there is eternal reward at the judgment severs the root of our bitterness. It reminds us that we do not seek earthly acclaim or temporal reward, which pass away; we seek lasting reward from God.

For several decades now, the doctrine of God's judgment has fallen into disrepute. It is rarely mentioned in Christian conversation or proclamation and is seen as offensive and off-putting to people. But it is a mistake to ignore this key doctrine. In the Bible, the doctrine of God's hatred of evil and his judgment of sin is often raised as a truth that should influence our behavior. Frequently, the prospect of reward for righteousness and punishment for unrighteousness is presented as an appeal for people to be wise in making the most important choices in life. The Scriptures are clear: there will be a final judgment, based on the decisions made in this life, and what happens at the judgment will seal our eternal destiny. In the parable about the sheep and the goats, Jesus mentions feeding the hungry, giving drink to the thirsty, welcoming the stranger, clothing the naked, visiting the sick, and going to see the prisoner as actions that will bring reward at the judgment (Matt. 25:35–36). He tells us that those who do not do these things will be punished (Matt. 25:42–43).

Asking people to consider the reality of future judgment as a motive to act lovingly is not a carrot that we dangle in front of them to inflame their selfishness, hoping that they will be motivated to seek personal gain from their acts of love. Rather, in light of the fact that our decisions impact eternity, we make it clear that a life of love is a worthwhile investment, one that is eternally secure. Jesus himself appealed to people in this way: "Do not lay up for yourselves treasures on earth, where moth and rust destroy and where thieves break in and steal, but lay up for yourselves treasures in heaven, where neither moth nor rust destroys and where thieves do not break in and steal" (Matt. 6:19–20). Clearly, Jesus felt that the desire for eternal reward, making investments in this life that will last for eternity, was a good motivation for our behavior.

, , ,

I am reminded of the story of Dr. Morrison, who was returning to the United States after a fruitful tour visiting many countries where he had preached the gospel to thousands of people. President Roosevelt was also on his ship, returning from a vacation in Africa. At the harbor in New York City there was a grand welcome for the President and a similar grand reception when he boarded a train. But no one had bothered to come to the harbor or the station to greet Dr. Morrison. As he boarded his train, the old baggage master happened to recognize him, saying "Hello, there!" in a casual sort of way.

Morrison recounts the growing bitterness in his heart: "I picked up my heavy gripes and started off, all alone. I could not help contrasting the homecoming of Roosevelt with my own. God had privileged me to lead ten thousand souls to Christ on that trip—and yet there I was, without a soul to meet me! Nobody cared. Suddenly I stopped. A new, glorious truth had gripped me. And I found myself saying aloud, slowly, exultantly, 'Maybe I'm not home yet! Maybe I'm not home!' "[8]

When we are tempted to lament our lack of recognition or reward, when the seeds of bitterness are taking root in our heart, we do well to remember that while a life of love may sometimes look like a waste of time and energy, it never fails to reap long-term rewards. We may not receive acclaim or honor in this life, but this life is not the end of the journey. As Dr. Morrison reminds us, we may not yet be home!

CHAPTER 8

ENVY VERSUS SHOWING HONOR

1 CORINTHIANS 13:4C

FROM THE BEGINNING, envy has been a problem for the human race. Cain, the eldest son of Adam and Eve, killed his brother Abel because he *envied* him. Cain was angry that Abel's sacrifice had been accepted by God while his own had been rejected (Gen. 4). I have no doubt that if we were able to uncover the reason behind many of the crises in the average local church, a large number of them would begin with the sin of envy.

Competition rules the world today. People no longer depend on one another to shape their identity and their sense of significance; instead, they are encouraged to "go it alone" and achieve their own individual pursuits. More often than not, our relationships are defined by rivalry, not charity. People who work on the same business team, and even many who serve in Christian ministry together, relate to one another as competitors in the quest for promotion and prominence.

The third characteristic of love that Paul writes about puts love in opposition to our tendency to envy others: "Love does *not* envy" (1 Cor. 13:4, emphasis added). The word we translate as "envy" in English is the Greek word *zē loō*. It is closely connected to the English word for "zeal,"[1] and in a positive sense, it means to be "deeply committed to something." A few verses earlier, in 1 Corinthians 12:31, Paul uses this word in a positive sense: "But earnestly desire [zēloō] the higher gifts." Now Paul uses the word in a negative way to indicate "strong envy and resentment against someone."[2]

We should remember, as I mentioned in the introduction, that this chapter on love is not a stand-alone passage. It is sandwiched between two chapters where Paul deals with the use and abuse of the certain gifts of the Spirit as speaking in tongues and prophecy. We can assume there were people in the Corinthian church who did not have these gifts, and they likely envied those who did.[3] In fact, Paul's entire letter paints a picture of a church in Corinth that is filled with party strife, an environment ripe for envy.

If envy is a problem that negates the power and impact of love, how do we learn to recognize it? Since envy is closely related to zeal and strong passion (yet in a negative way), it can be seen in the extent to which people are willing to go when someone else is recognized or receives something they feel they deserve.

- A professor rejected for the post of dean at an academic institution responds by resigning from the institution.
- A church member is given the job of reading the announcements at church, and others say she was chosen because she curried favor with the pastor by giving gifts to his children.
- A highly talented newcomer joins a committee, and the other people on the committee react negatively to her, fearing that she will become more prominent than them.
- A teenage girl is filled with anger toward another teenager who receives numerous compliments because she is attractive.
- Someone who worked hard for a program is not mentioned when those who helped are publicly thanked, while several people who did not work hard are mentioned. He is angry over the omission and spends a lot of time and energy trying to highlight the short-comings of the people who were mentioned.
- When a child is overlooked for the key role in a Christmas play, the parents stop coming to church in disgust.

This envy is expressed in ways that cause conflict and unpleasantness among God's people. And that causes God to be dishonored, which is the greatest tragedy that can happen on earth. But those responsible for dishonoring God are so blinded by their rage that they do not realize the damage they are doing. Many of them think instead that they are in a legitimate battle for establishing justice in the church.

COMPARISON BREEDS ANGER

American preacher-teacher Howard Hendricks has said, "Comparison is the favorite indoor sport of Christians."[4] Comparison is particularly rampant in our age, which pushes people to think about others as competitors. The whole nature of education today is based on competition. We have spelling competitions, debating competitions, and athletic competitions. And those who excel get praised. There is a good side to competition, because it can push us to do our best. But there is a bad side, since it can lead to envy and even worse. The result of being compared to others, especially in childhood, is that envy becomes part of our nature and we begin to look at others with hostility.

What is unique about us is the *combination* of characteristics that go into our being who we are. In God's sight we are unique and just as important and significant as anyone else in the body of Christ, as Paul is at pains to show in 1 Corinthians 12. So there is no reason for us to envy anybody. But we can always find somebody who is better than we are in some of the individual characteristics that go into making us the unique persons we are. What is special about us is the combination of characteristics. So, to build our sense of self-worth, if we compare ourselves with a few characteristics of other people, we will always be unhappy.

I'll add to this a warning to parents and those in leadership. You may have had parents or mentors who motivated you to succeed by using comparison. They always measured you and your success or failure by comparing you with others. If this was true in your life, you are likely to do the same with your own children and with those that you lead. You must learn to battle consciously against this natural tendency you have to compare your children or those you lead with other people.

When a child comes home from school and shares how he did on his exams, his results should be compared against his own abilities and progress measured by his own improvement, not by how well he compares to others. We should avoid questions like, "How did your cousin John do?" When parents use comparison with siblings to motivate their children, an inner wound can develop that often surfaces later in life. Parents must then live with the sad reality that their children do not live in harmony with each other. Statements like, "Why can't you be like your sister?" contribute to an unhealthy pattern in children that they carry with them, long after they have grown into adulthood.

What is the alternative? We should always look at others through the eyes of love—of what is best for them. We rejoice when someone does well and are sad when someone does badly. If your daughter's marriage is unhappy, you should be unhappy about it. But if the marriage of your sister's daughter is a happy one, you can truly rejoice over it. There is no need to compare the two relationships. The sadness you feel in one case and the happiness you feel in the other are both rooted in your love for each person.

OVERCOMING ENVY WITH LOVE

If we understand who we are in Christ and something of the significant role he has given us in his agenda, we would not have a reason to envy anyone. This is such an important issue that we will give the whole of the next chapter to it. But here let me point to Paul's instruction: " ... in humility count others more significant [or 'better' — NRSV] than yourselves" (Phil. 2:3). Everyone has something they are better at than us. Without being envious, out of the strength of the significance God has given us, we can joyfully recognize the significance of something in which someone else excels. Let me suggest a new ambition for you to cultivate: look for significant things about others and rejoice in them. This is the attitude of someone who loves, as Paul alludes to a few verses later: "Love ... does not rejoice at wrongdoing, but rejoices with the truth. Love ... believes all things, hopes all things" (1 Cor. 13:6–7).

Paul gives a similar challenge to us in Romans 12:10 when he tells us to "outdo one another in showing honor." Here is a form of competition that the Bible endorses: competing to show honor to others, more than they show honor to you! This is a practical way to apply the principle that Paul is teaching: "Do not be overcome by evil, but overcome evil with good" (12:21). One of the best ways we can overcome the evil of envy is by showing honor to the very person we are tempted to envy.

All of this is well illustrated in a story from the life of Samuel Chadwick, the great British Methodist preacher. Before he was known as a prominent preacher, Chadwick was invited to speak at a conference along with G. Campbell Morgan, a man Chadwick considered to be "easily the best known preacher in the English language." He writes: "I thought, what an honor to be speaking on the same program with G. Campbell Morgan! Perhaps, some folks are taking notice of me!" The two preachers were scheduled to speak back-to-back daily at alternate times.

On the first morning Chadwick spoke to a large crowd for the first hour and then Morgan followed him, speaking to a comparable crowd the second hour. The next morning, Morgan spoke to a large crowd, but when Chadwick rose to speak, many people left the room. The next morning Chadwick spoke first, to a small group, and again was followed by Morgan, who drew a much larger audience.

Chadwick was hurt by the response of the crowds. He went to his room to be alone and he prayed, "This is not fair, Lord." As he laid his bruised ego before the Lord, he felt God asking him a question. "Are you sorry, Chadwick, that we've got a fellow like Morgan on our team?" Chadwick thought about it for a moment. "No," he said to the Lord, "but it hurts!" Then he felt God asking him again: "Are you suggesting that I quit blessing Morgan?"

Chadwick immediately realized the folly of his envious heart. "Forgive my attitude, Lord," he prayed. "No, I am not sorry we've got a fellow like this on our team, and I don't want you to quit blessing him." For the rest of the conference, Chadwick blocked out a time to pray for Morgan and for the success of his ministry. He said, "After that, I found myself going with excitement to hear Morgan each day, giving thanks that we had a fellow like that on our team."[5]

What a liberating gift we have in the ability to bless others! By praying for them, the very people we are prone to envy can become a source of joy for us. Their success can become our success, as we celebrate what the Lord is doing through them. There is no longer a concern for our own name, which leads to unhealthy competition and envy, but we are freed to do our best for God.

That is what all of us must do. We should not be motivated to pursue excellence by competing with others, but by a vision for the glory of God. Our desire to see God's name lifted up and praised should lead us to reflect the excellence of the God we serve by using the gifts he has given us to the best of our abilities. Even then, we must live in light of the gospel, acknowledging that we will often fail, but that our acceptance before God is not based on how well we perform but on the performance of Christ alone. We continue to do our best, using our gifts and talents wisely and serving with a zeal and passion that are based on a firm grasp of God's love for us and our love for God.

ENCOURAGING VICTORIOUS RIVALS

Moses deeply desired the joy of leading his people into the Promised Land, the land west of the Jordan River. However, because of some rash leadership decisions he made, God did not allow him this honor. Moses frequently mentions his desire to enter (see Deut. 1:38). Once, he "pleaded with the LORD" about this, saying: "Please let me go over and see the good land beyond the Jordan" (3:23, 25).

But God's response to Moses was clear, "Enough from you; do not speak to me of this matter again" (Deut 3:26). Instead, Moses was asked to commission Joshua for this task, to introduce him to the people and to encourage him to faithfully lead the people into the land of promise (1:38; 3:28; all of ch. 31). Moses was being asked to train and promote the very man who had been given his "dream job," the man who would get to do what he had longed to do ever since becoming Israel's leader. Scripture does not record any sense of envy or jealously that Moses felt toward Joshua. Rather, he performed all of his tasks faithfully, as one called to serve the Lord.

Or consider the example of Jonathan, the son of King Saul. The pattern of succession in most nations in the ancient world was for the son to succeed his father as king. But instead of following this pattern, God rejected Saul and chose David instead. Though David took much of the glory that would have typically gone to Jonathan, David and Jonathan became firm friends. In fact, Jonathan did all he could to protect David from his father Saul's mad schemes to destroy him. First Samuel 20 records how Jonathan defended David before Saul, making his father so angry that he hurled a spear at Jonathan. After this incident Jonathan warned David to flee to safety.

While many people may want to be in a position of leadership, the truth is that only one person can be appointed to that role. It is inevitable that some who aspire to the job will be rejected. Sometimes, the person chosen may be younger or have less experience than another person who is passed over. While seniority and experience are important criteria, giftedness, wisdom, and ability are also important considerations. Sometimes, a younger person may actually be the better candidate for a particular role or position, while at other times an older person may be the best choice. Either way, once a decision is made, the rejected person should join in, give the new leader his full backing, and even be willing to encourage the new leader in his job. The importance of our position is nothing in comparison with the importance of God's agenda. Our ultimate commitment is to see his agenda fulfilled, not our own ambitions. The disappointment of rejection is nothing when we are consumed by an ambition to glorify God.

Sadly, this is not always the response we see. One person is chosen instead of another, and the rejected leader stages a protest that brings division and turmoil to the group. They may seek redress in the courts and challenge the decision. Or they may seek to undermine the person chosen by pointing out all of his shortcomings. When this happens, God's name is dishonored, precious time is lost, and the progress of the kingdom of God is hindered. Even if the decision was wrong, God will not allow something of ultimate detriment to the kingdom of God to last forever. If we respond to these decisions in a Christlike way, even "wrong" decisions can become a means of God doing a greater work of good in our lives.

, , , ,

Many battles have been waged in the history of the church over issues of justice, doctrine, or strategy—when all too often the real reason for the disagreement is simply envy. We must be careful that our zeal for God is real and is not just a mask to hide our own selfish ambitions motivated by envy for others.

In their futile efforts to gain honor for themselves, some people actually hurt themselves and dishonor the name of God. How liberating it is, instead, to concentrate on loving our rivals and blessing them. God is honored, we receive an eternal reward for it, and we enjoy the happiness and satisfaction of being able to rest in the security and approval that God gives to us in Jesus—not in our own efforts to be noticed, praised, or honored. The rewards we receive in this world will fade and pass away, but the reward we receive at the judgment will last forever.

CHAPTER 9

ACCEPTING WHO WE ARE: THE ANTIDOTE TO ENVY

1 CORINTHIANS 13:4C

IN HIS CLASSIC BOOK *Knowing God,* J. I. Packer asks the question, "What is a Christian?" He answers it by saying, "The richest answer I know is that a Christian is one who has God for his Father."[1] He continues: "You sum up the whole of New Testament teaching in a single phrase, if you speak of it as a revelation of the fatherhood of the holy Creator."[2] The apostle John expresses his amazement over this truth when he says, "See what kind of love the Father has given to us, that we should be called children of God; and so we are" (1 John 3:1). We are adopted children of our heavenly Father, and at the heart of our acceptance as his adopted children is the grace that flows through the work of Christ, freely given to us despite our unworthiness. The grace of God elevates us from being enemies of God, people dead in our sins and trespasses, to a beloved position as princes and princesses in the kingdom of God.

In the previous chapter we reflected on Paul's statement that "love does not envy" (13:4). Now we must look at a root cause for envy: an uncertainty about one's own self-worth. Many Christians do not feel accepted by God, or they struggle to receive his love for them. As a result, they become insecure, not experiencing the identity and significance of being children of God that the Bible speaks of. Without this security, others become a threat to them and the result is envy. If Christians understand the identity God gives them as his children and the significance he gives them through the work he calls them to do, they should have no need to envy anyone. Out of the strength of our identity and significance, both of which are gifts given to us by God and received in faith, we can be freed from envy to appreciate the successes of other people.

The problem we all face is that *we know the truth of our identity and significance in our heads, but we do not sense it in our hearts.* The journey from the head to the heart can be long and complex, requiring us to repeatedly open ourselves up to the healing work of God's Spirit. I find that many devout Christians continue to struggle with a sense of inadequacy. This problem becomes a major hindrance to exercising Christian love and instead triggers envy. So we will devote this whole chapter to discussing how we can overcome it.

HOW GOD SEES US

The descriptions we have in Scripture that tell us how God sees us are nothing less than breathtaking. Consider just a sample of verses that describe the delight that God has when he looks at us (emphasis added).

- "Great is the LORD, who *delights* in the welfare of his servant!" (Ps. 35:27)
- "Our steps are made firm by the LORD, when he *delights* in our way." (Ps. 37:23 NRSV)
- "The LORD *delights* in those who fear him, who put their hope in his unfailing love." (Ps. 147:11 NIV)
- "For the LORD takes *delight* in his people; he crowns the humble with victory." (Ps. 149:4 NIV)

Zephaniah 3:17 is a personal favorite for me: "The LORD your God is in your midst, a mighty one who will save; he will rejoice over you with gladness; he will quiet you by his love; he will exult over you with loud singing." Just think of what this means! The almighty God, the Lord of the universe, exults over you with loud singing. You make him happy because you are his treasured possession. When I think of this, I picture a happy father who is watching his little girl performing in a drama at her school. He is so pleased and excited by what she is doing that he spontaneously cries out in approval and praise, not caring what those around him may think: "That's my girl!"

Children need such messages of affirmation from their family members. Sharing appreciation and praise for God's goodness and his gifts should be as normal a part of our lives as breathing and eating. This is why God asks and even commands us to praise him. It's not that he is lacking anything. God does not feel empty without our praise, nor is he in need of our approval. He commands our praise because the joy of our relationship with him is *incomplete* until it is expressed in our praise. Praise and affirmation of God are the end product—the consummation—of our love for him.

We can extend this "theology" of praise to our human relationships as well. The Song of Songs reminds us that men and women should study their spouses, meditate on what they appreciate about them, and express the fruit of their study in words. This love poem is filled with praise and appreciation for the beauty, character, and gifts of the husband and wife in their marriage relationship.

Sadly, however, the type of affirmation that God gives to us and that we see expressed in the Song of Songs is not the norm. Many Christian children grow up without ever hearing the affirming words of their parents' joy over what they have done and who they are. Instead, they hear a constant refrain that they've got to *do better*, that they've got to *try harder*, and that they just are *not good enough*. Children must be challenged to pursue excellence, but that push to succeed must be balanced with good doses of praise and encouragement. Those who have not been affirmed in their childhood may grow up to be successful, rich, and powerful. But they won't be happy because they do not have a sense of being loved and accepted. The joy of being accepted by God is the greatest wealth one can have.

A lack of genuine affirmation can also result in stunted spiritual growth. Having not experienced affirmation, some may find it difficult to understand that God truly looks at them with joy and approval. They struggle to hear and accept this truth, even when they are affirmed because their personalities are not geared to accepting affirmation. They may know the truth about their adoption as a child of God in their heads, but in their hearts they do not enjoy its benefits. Having never learned what it means to be truly loved, their hearts are not able to fully relish the joy of being loved and accepted by God.

Experiencing fully the riches of our identity and significance in Christ can be a challenge for any Christian. For most, this is a path of discovery that we will travel on until we meet the Lord face-to-face. Only in heaven will we be totally freed from the ravages of sin and the power of false values that have shaped us and are still powerfully at work in the world around.

FIVE KEYS TO HELP US GROW

I will now present five keys that I believe can help us to grow in our understanding that we have a new identity and an eternal significance as God's children.

1. SATURATING OURSELVES IN THE WORD

Several years ago, around the time I was preparing to give a series of messages on 2 Corinthians 5, I received a British visa that had an expiration date prior to my proposed date of entry to England. Obviously, this would not work, so I had to write a letter to the British High Commissioner, explaining my problem and trying to get a fresh visa without having to pay the high visa fees again.

I was quite surprised to get a nice letter back from him and was relieved to find that the problem had been quickly solved. I remembered that I had addressed the British Ambassador as "Your Excellency." At the time I happened to be studying a verse in 2 Corinthians that talked about the fact that we are "ambassadors for Christ" (2 Cor. 5:20). Suddenly, the thought came to me: "I am calling this person 'Your Excellency' because he is the Ambassador of the Queen of Britain. Yet I am an Ambassador of the *King* of the Queen of Britain!"

The Bible is loaded with texts that describe our rich identity and significance. We are often described as God's *children* (John 1:12; Gal. 4:4–5; Eph. 1:4–5; 1 John 3:1). Earlier in this chapter we saw five verses that talk about God delighting over us. Paul says that "if [we are] children, then [we are] heirs — heirs of God and fellow heirs with Christ, provided we suffer with him in order that we may also be glorified with him" (Rom. 8:17). Neil T. Anderson has helpfully popularized the idea that we should take time to affirm these statements about who we are, making lists of passages that we can memorize as God's therapy to the bondages that bind us and cause us to miss out on God's best for our lives.[3]

Some of the amazing and out-of-this-world things the Bible says about us should bring a constant smile to our face. Yet sadly, these great and amazing truths usually don't affect the way we think and act. We may have kept them in our minds as biblical information, but they do not affect our attitudes.

The journey from the mind to the heart is sometimes a long and difficult one. Sokreaksa (Reaksa) Himm lived during the time of the "Killing Fields" in Cambodia under the rule of the Khmer Rouge led by Pol Pot. Reaksa, as he was commonly known, was scheduled, along with his family, for elimination by this oppressive and evil regime. He saw his father and most of his family killed, and he himself was brutally clubbed and left for dead. In all, eleven members of his family as well as a sister-in-law and nephew were killed. Reaksa was thirteen years old at the time all of this happened.

Somehow, he managed to recover from the beating he had received and escaped, but before leaving the mass grave in which he had lain with his dead family members for several hours, he made three promises to them: "Mother, father, brothers and sisters, as long as I live, I will try to avenge your deaths. If I fail in this, then I promise that I'll become a monk. If I can't fulfill these promises, then I won't live in Cambodia any more."[4]

Some years later, Reaksa went to a refugee camp in Thailand, where he met Jesus Christ. Subsequently, he traveled to Canada, and the long painful process of healing began. Therapists told him that he had an extreme case of Post-Traumatic Stress Disorder (PTSD). Helped by others, Reaksa began to make determined progress along the road to healing.

One of the first signs of his progress was learning to cry. Reaksa continued to struggle with recurring nightmares that had haunted him for many years, and during this time, he found the book of Psalms to be a wonderful source of support and comfort. He writes, "Here [in the Psalms] was someone like me who had known despair, and who was not afraid to cry out to God in pain and anguish." He began to read a psalm every day, and, he says, "as I read, my trust in God's goodness and power was strengthened. I felt more secure."

Psalm 23 became his favorite psalm. "Whenever I read it, I felt safe in the presence of God."[5] Reaksa began to use this psalm as a daily evening meditation; soon, the nightmares stopped. Not once did he dream "about being hunted by the Khmer Rouge and the Thai soldiers." Reaksa wrote, "It seems as though my need for security and comfort while I sleep is met by this psalm, because I know I can trust God."[6] Eventually, Reaksa broke his third promise to his family, traveling back to Cambodia. Today, he is involved in bringing healing to those who, like him, suffered during that terrible period in Cambodia's history.

The story of Reaksa reminds us that the Word of God is powerful, and it can counteract the evil messages that come to us from the world. We need to allow the Word to do its work in us. Admittedly, this can take time. We must dedicate time to reading the Scriptures, meditating on them, memorizing them, and challenging ourselves by preaching to our souls. Listening to the preaching of the Word can also have a helpful effect on our hearts and minds.

2. THE WITNESS OF THE SPIRIT

In Romans 8:15–17, the apostle Paul explicitly grapples with questions of our identity. He begins by describing our status as children of God: "For you did not receive the spirit of slavery to fall back into fear, but you have received the Spirit of adoption as sons, by whom we cry, 'Abba! Father!'" (Rom. 8:15).

Yet while we may know this to be true, that we are children of our heavenly Father, we still wonder: How do we make this truth real in our *experience*? Thankfully, the next verse suggests the answer. It is through the working of the Spirit: "The Spirit himself bears witness with our spirit that we are children of God" (Rom. 8:16; see also Gal. 4:6). Through different experiences the Holy Spirit does his work of convincing us that we are, indeed, God's children.

He can do this in several different ways:

- When we read the Scriptures inspired by the Holy Spirit, he convinces us through them of our position as children.
- We may be providentially exposed to a passage from Scripture or a message given in a way that speaks directly to our situation. Our scheduled reading for a particular day, something said in a message at a service we attend, or a letter that comes in the mail seems to give us exactly what we need to hear in that moment. We realize that the seeming coincidence we now have was orchestrated by the Holy Spirit, to encourage us and remind us that God loves us.
- A similar kind of conviction can come about through God's amazing providence, where he supplies us with something we desperately need at just the right time.

These types of experiences, when taken together with the truth of God that we hear in Scripture, help us to grasp at an experiential, heart level that God is personally interested in us as individuals. That makes it easier for us to believe that God views us as his precious children.

3. LINGERING IN THE PRESENCE OF GOD

Over the years I have found great inspiration in reading about and studying the lives of other Christians. I have many heroes who inspire my faith, but high up on the list is the British pastor, scholar, and church leader John Stott. I have grown up reading Stott's books, and his writings have provided me with a good model of how to preach and think biblically.

I first met Stott in the mid–1970s when I was a student at Fuller Seminary in California. During his visit to the seminary, I attended every program in which he was involved. At one point, there was a question-and-answer session; when it was finished, Dr. Stott walked up to me and asked, "Do I know you, brother?" "No," I said, "but you know my parents." Dr. Stott had been to Sri Lanka while I was in the United States attending school, and he had come to know my parents during that visit. I vividly remember that when we finished talking, he gave me a great big hug! For the next few days, I think I floated several feet above the ground. I felt incredibly special, having been blessed to receive affirmation from someone I respected so much.

Something similar can happen when we slow down and spend unhurried time in God's presence. Great security and joy, along with fresh affirmation of our standing as children of God, come from being in his presence. We begin to imbibe the truth of Moses' words, "The eternal God is your dwelling place, and underneath are the everlasting arms" (Deut. 33:27).

A daily dose of such security has a way of changing our perception of ourselves. Sadly, however, instead of prayer people turn to activity for their identity. Their work becomes too important to them. Some become restless souls, afraid to stop or slow down their frantic pace and busy activity. They work without taking a break because they sense that stopping will force them to confront the emptiness of their hearts. To avoid this, when they do stop to take a break, they enter an imaginary world offered by TV or some other pastime.

These experiences, though they can be good when experienced in moderation, are never a substitute for silence in the presence of God. Overwork, when combined with insecurity, makes a person a prime candidate for burnout. Some will become possessive of the work. They will feel threatened by others and won't be comfortable delegating responsibilities. When they need to finally let go and hand over their responsibility to another, they find they cannot do it. Still others grow bitter or angry. They see what they do as *their* work, not God's work. Consequently, their identity is based on their success rather than on God's acceptance of them. Because they are not living a life rooted in the love and acceptance of God, there is a constant need to prove themselves. They feel insecure and are threatened by the success of others.

When I feel insecure or threatened, or find myself in a hostile environment, I find it helpful to slip away, be with God for a few minutes, recharge my batteries, and remind myself that I am a servant who serves under the authority of my Master. If I cannot slip away physically, I try to do so mentally. Even when I am in the midst of a stressful conflict situation, I try to become more conscious of God's presence. This gives me peace and helps me not to react rashly or out of irritation.

In Psalm 34, David writes, "Those who look to him [God] are radiant" (Ps. 34:5). When we gaze into the beauty of God (see 27:4), we begin to radiate some of his glory. When Moses came down from Mount Sinai, having spent several days in the presence of God, "the skin of his face shone because he had been talking with God" (Exod. 34:29).

Paul picks up on the experience of Moses in his second letter to the Corinthians when he alludes to Moses' experience on Mount Sinai and the request of the people that Moses veil his shining face. Paul writes: "And we all, with unveiled face, beholding the glory of the Lord, are being transformed into the same image from one degree of glory to another" (2 Cor. 3:18). Those who linger in the presence of God will naturally begin to radiate something of his glory in a way that will be evident to others. David gives us a hint as to how this happens, telling us that "their faces shall never be ashamed" (Ps. 34:5). In other words, one of the ways in which we radiate the glory of God is by *grasping the truth of our acceptance before him*. Feelings of inferiority disappear as we unite afresh with God and dwell in his love for us. The power of shame no longer has hold over our lives.

4. THE WORK GOD HAS GIVEN US

As a child I often felt depressed. I didn't think I was good at anything. I had brothers who were excellent athletes or who excelled in their academic studies. Honestly, I was mediocre in both of these areas. I began to believe that I was the one child in my family who would never amount to anything. I certainly did not experience much joy knowing that I was a child of God.

In my early teens, however, I began to walk more closely with God. Almost immediately, I sensed a desire to preach. I dared not tell anyone about my sense of calling because I thought they would laugh at me. After all, I rarely opened my mouth in public. I was sure that people would find it strange that I, of all people, would want to be a preacher! Still, the desire continued to grow in my heart, and I began to write a sermon every week.

When a friend of mine moved to an area where there were no churches, I started mailing my weekly sermon to him.

The burden to preach grew so heavy on me that I began going to the beach close to my home at night when no one else was around. I would sit on a rock and preach to the sea breeze. Then, in my later teens people sensed that I had something of a gift, and I began to have opportunities to preach to real people. Even after forty-six years, I can honestly say that the thrill of preaching has never left me! I share this because the call to preach has had a significant impact on my life. It convinced me of my significance before God. Though I already knew I was a child of God, I did not begin to experience the thrill of this truth until I grasped that my heavenly Father had given me a gift, a gift he could use for his glory.

Paul tells us that God gifts the members of the body of Christ with abilities that are specific to them. Each person in the body has a significant niche or responsibility that only they can fill. Paul writes, "All these are empowered by one and the same Spirit, who apportions to each one individually as he wills" (1 Cor. 12:11). The Holy Spirit "apportions" or "distributes" (NIV) to each one what is best suited for the individual.

In the verses that follow (12:12–31), Paul shows us that each gift is significant, and there is no place for inferiority or superiority complexes in the body of Christ. In two other gifts-related passages Paul uses the term "measure" (Rom. 12:3; Eph. 4:7; Gk. *metron*), again stressing that there has been a careful apportioning (or measuring out) of the gifts by the Holy Spirit. When we understand this, there is no need to envy anybody because we know that we have a part to play that is unique and significant. One of the key responsibilities of leaders is to help those they lead to understand what their gifts are and how to use those gifts. Parents and leaders must work to foster a culture where all gifts are treated as equally significant.

5. ACCEPTANCE BY THE COMMUNITY OF BELIEVERS

We tend to think that costly commitment to others is just too inconvenient today. Jesus once talked about the "hired hand" shepherd who leaves the sheep and runs away when the wolf comes (John 10:12). Unfortunately, what Jesus describes is far too common today.

Jesus gave us a model for how we should treat others in the family of God, telling his followers that he is the "good shepherd [who] lays down his life for the sheep" (John 10:11). The sacrificial, suffering death of Jesus is our model for how we should seek to treat others in the family of God. Jesus instructs us: "Love one another as I have loved you. Greater love has no one than this, that someone lay down his life for his friends" (John 15:12–13).

If we, as a church, loved others with just a fraction of this radical love, I believe it would have an incredible impact for eternity. New believers who come to Christ with a history of deep hurt would discover significance as they experience love and acceptance by other Christians. They will begin to believe they are lovable, and this experience of being loved in Christian community will open their hearts to receive the truth that they are loveable people. This in turn makes it possible for them to accept that God loves them. Throughout the centuries, millions have come to understand God's great love for them through the gateway of Christian love.

, , ,

As important as it is to affirm the giftedness of individuals to serve God and to communicate that people are accepted in Christian community, we must never forget that these things cannot be the ultimate source of our identity and significance. Using the gifts God has given us to serve and receiving affirmation and praise from others can be helpful, but neither of these can serve as the root of our security. Seeking our identity and significance from other Christians or from our own ability to serve, preach, or minister to others will leave us disillusioned and disappointed. Inevitably, our fellow Christians will hurt us. We will have days when our ministry feels dead and our gifts seem to fail us.

But if our significance comes from God, we will stand secure on the solid rock of God's Word, knowing that we are free to love because we are the beloved of God. Our gifts and the Christian community open us to accepting and understanding God's affirmation. But we should not stop there. We should go through the open door afforded through gifts and community and graduate to finding our significance and identity primarily from God.

Strangely enough, I've met Christians who don't want to change. They prefer to cling to their wounds, rooting their identity in the fact that they have been hurt, that others have disappointed them, that they have not been treated as they thought they deserved. They are angry about life, and their anger leads them to respond as a victim, which gives them an excuse for their negative thoughts. They may also be blind to the sin of envy in their heart because their bondage to this sin reinforces their conviction that the world and the church owe them. In the end, they condemn themselves to an unhappy life and spread their unhappiness to others.

Each of us ultimately has a choice to make. Will we believe what God's Word says about us so that we can experience the great treasures of our identity and significance? Or will we cling to the idea that life has been bad to us, refuse God's healing, and miss experiencing our identity and significance? The former choice will open the door to joy and a life of love. The latter will condemn us to discontent and envy.

CHAPTER 10

SHARING WITHOUT BOASTING

1 CORINTHIANS 13:4D

AS WE HAVE NOTED, there were some people in the church of Corinth who lacked certain gifts of the Spirit, and they envied those who had these gifts. So Paul reminds them (and us) that love does not *envy*.

But it is likely that some of those who had such gifts were guilty of the opposite problem—they boasted about their gifts to those who didn't have them.[1] Paul's opponents also were guilty of boasting, highlighting their own speaking abilities or flaunting their insights and teachings in such a way that the people in Corinth began to lose their esteem for the apostle Paul and his teachings.[2] Paul gently reminds the church that boasting is not consistent with love: "Love does not ... boast" (1 Cor. 13:4).

The verb we translate "boast" in this passage literally means "to heap praise on oneself."[3] Today some people are not ashamed to show off their abilities, achievements, and possessions, and they do so without anyone expressing reservations about what they are doing. Even preachers who boast about their abilities and achievements can attract large crowds through their boasting. Yet Paul is clear that boasting is not acceptable for Christians.

SHARING OUR VICTORIES

Boasting is *not* the same as sharing our victories with others. Elsewhere, Paul asks us to "rejoice with those who rejoice" (Rom. 12:15), and he says that "if one member is honored, all rejoice together" (1 Cor. 12:26). They would not know to rejoice with us unless we tell them. Our joy is not complete until it is shared with others, and one of the best things about friendship is that we can share our joys with our friends. A student who has just received an excellent score on an important examination doesn't simply go into his room, close the door, and say to himself, "I passed; I passed; I passed!" No! He shares his achievement with others.

Sharing our victories with others can be a loving thing. When people love one another, they enjoy sharing in victories together. Of course, it requires wisdom to know *when* we should share these things, *how* we should do it, and with *whom* to share. With some we share everything, with others we may share a few things, and with still others we may decide not to share anything, knowing that it will not lead to their edification or enjoyment.

A young man who does well on his exams should be somewhat restrained about his joy when he is talking to a person who is disappointed over his failure on the same exam. But in sharing with his parents, he can share his joy with them and invite them to celebrate his good news. Our sharing is an act of love when it leads to an increase of mutual joy and brings encouragement to others. If sharing is unlikely to increase joy or bring encouragement, we should consider keeping silent out of love for the other person.

SHARING TESTIMONIES

On some Sundays we have testimonies shared in the worship service at our church. Earlier we used to invite anyone who wanted to share a testimony to come up and share from the platform. Usually a few people volunteered every Sunday. But we soon found that some of the testimonies were shared in such as way as to bring honor to the sharer and to show what a good Christian he or she was. So we decided to stop asking for volunteers. Now when we know that someone has a story that will edify others, we ask them to share it at the service.

Boasting is sharing in a way that will show that we are better than others, or we showcase our talents or dedication in a way that will bring honor to us. In one sense, this is natural, for some people have had wonderful experiences and want others to have the same experience. But they may share about it in a way that makes others feel small for not having such an experience. This probably happened with those who had these special gifts in Corinth. Certainly this has happened in the modern charismatic movement when a new manifestation, like "holy laughter," appeared and some Christians experienced it. They judged others based on whether they too had experienced this. We can be grateful that such people usually get more balanced after a period of time and become more sensitive to their hearers when they share what they have experienced.

William Barclay tells the story of a man who visited his doctor and was informed that his heart was tired and he must rest. He phoned his employer, who was a well-known Christian, with the news. The Christian leader answered: "I have an inward strength which enables me to carry on."[4] This was a testimony given without love. At a time when he should have listened to, sympathized with, and comforted his employee, he shared a testimony that made the employee feel small. It brought more pain to an already suffering person.

Biblical testimonies come out of gratitude to God for what he has done to us. Gratitude and pride do not usually get on well together. Gratitude focuses on someone else, whereas pride focuses on self. When we understand grace, we realize that we have done nothing to merit it. But that does not make us feel small. It fills us with joy, for the eternal God has treated us like his children. Grace gives us an exalted identity. With the strength of this we can concentrate on lifting others up rather than ourselves. Interestingly, many times when people boast about something, they start their comments with words something like, "I'm so humbled." The sharing, however, gives no hint of humility.

Sometimes people are so eager to share their testimony that they don't realize that they are causing an inconvenience to the other person, who may be in a hurry to do something else. Our desire is to be a blessing to people, not just to share what is on our heart. At other times, when we have begun a testimony, someone else may butt in and tell his or her story. We should not have to feel bad that we could not tell our story; that is not one of the essentials of life. The essential is love, which makes us want people to be blessed. And if they are blessed by another person's experience, we should rejoice.

SHARING ABOUT OUR ACHIEVEMENTS AND SERVICE

The great Scottish pastor-theologian James Denney (1856–1917), recognizing the inherent danger of pride and boasting in leading a worship service, had the following statement framed in the vestry from which he went to lead the worship service: "No man can bear witness to Christ and himself at the same time. No man can give the impression that he himself is clever and that Christ is mighty to save."[5]

Good words to remember anytime we speak, sing, or preach!

Jesus taught his disciples that we need not boast in our accomplishments or our acts of service. He said to them, "But when you give to the needy, do not let your left hand know what your right hand is doing, so that your giving may be in secret. And your Father who sees in secret will reward you" (Matt. 6:3–4). In the world, companies today may give large sums of money to needy causes. Sometimes, this is done because the owners or shareholders truly value the cause. In other cases, it is done in the hope of gaining some marketing benefit from the sponsorship. Though this may be standard practice in the business world, in our personal lives we do not follow this practice. If God knows that we have given money or served a cause, that is enough for us.

Of course, this does not mean that we should try to hide our efforts to help others. Often, it is helpful and necessary to let the people we help *know* we are helping them. That is one way we experience partnership with those we help. But we aren't concerned with reward for our effort. If we know that our "Father who sees in secret will reward" us, we will be satisfied.

I am often invited to speak at conferences, and one of the least pleasant aspects is listening to people give long descriptions of what they are doing. It's not that I dislike listening to stories, and some of the stories I hear are truly inspiring and challenging. But at other times, the stories are simply an opportunity for people to promote themselves. I usually end up responding to the inspiring stories by saying something like, "How wonderful God is" or "How good it is to be serving God." The long stories that boast about achievements do not bring such inspiration to the hearers.

We must guard carefully against the temptation to take to ourselves the glory that belongs to God alone. This can easily happen when we are involved in a public ministry like speaking or performing music. When we preach or perform, our primary aim is that the message gets through, that people are blessed, and, in the case of worship, that people are led to the throne of God. We must ensure that we do not try to make an impression with our music or speaking or whatever in such a way that it detracts from the good that the program should achieve.

My friend Ramez Atallah now serves as General Secretary of the Bible

Society of Egypt. He went as a "youth delegate" to the famous 1974 International Congress on World Evangelization in Lausanne, Switzerland, and at this conference he was part of a small group that met daily. Over the ten days of the conference, the members of his group got to know each other well. Each day, they shared their stories and something about their ministries.

One of those in Ramez's group was a man named Festo Orlang. He shared with the group how he had been an unregenerate school teacher who had been converted in the East African revival. He had many children, some born before his conversion and some after. He said that those born before his conversion had suffered greatly, but those born after his conversion were far more blessed. An older lady in his church would serve him by rebuking him if he failed to act in a Christlike manner. He shared how he was grateful for her influence in his life. As this group met each day, Festo would give instances of how God had humbled him because he was such a proud person.

At the end of the conference the members of this small group shared their visiting cards with each other. Ramez put Festo's card into his pocket, not bothering to look at it. On his flight home, Ramez took out the various cards he had gathered and began to read them. When he came to Festo's card, he read: "Festo Orlang, Archbishop of Kenya." My friend Ramez had assumed that this man was simply the pastor of a small congregation in rural Kenya. Yet here was the leader of one of the largest branches of the Anglican church—overseeing the life of approximately three million people! Festo had not felt it necessary to tell his group members that he was the archbishop of his country. Love does not boast for one simple reason: *because it is focused on lifting up God and others.*

We cannot overcome boasting by trying *not* to focus on ourselves. We overcome boasting by looking at God and how good he has been to us. We cannot root out pride by trying *not* to be proud; we allow our pride to be overwhelmed by God's grace. Having being raised up to such a height in Christ, we find that we want nothing more than to lift up the name of God and serve others. We are no longer upset when we are not recognized because we know that God recognizes us. We aren't seeking to be known by others because we understand that we are known by God.

, , ,

In various places in his letters, and especially in 2 Corinthians 10 – 12, Paul makes a list of the work he has done and how much he has suffered.

Was it his goal to boast, to prove to others that he was somehow deserving of his position as an apostle and leader in the church? Not at all. Paul admits he has no desire to talk about these things, but he felt that it was necessary to share the truth because he was under attack and because the gospel he had preached was being undermined by false teachers.

Paul was responding to specific accusations with clear answers, and his motive was love. He was seeking to defend the gospel for the sake of the purity of the church, and that meant countering the false stories that others had spread about him. As we see in his example, when sharing about ourselves or highlighting the blessings we have received from God, our motivation should be love for others. We speak the truth in love. Our desire is to foster the good of the people we serve, not to boost our own reputation.

CHAPTER 11

ARROGANCE: A SIGN OF WEAKNESS

1 CORINTHIANS 13:4D

ONE OF THE MOST common allegations I hear people make today is that Christians are arrogant. I'm always dismayed to hear this because an attitude of arrogance should be foreign to the Christian faith. Yet sadly, these allegations are not made without reason.

Arrogance involves looking down on others, assuming that we hold a position of superiority over them. In Sri Lanka, I hear people say things like: "My daughter will not marry a man from that family/caste/class." Or someone will look at another person and say, "He is an uneducated person. He dropped out of school without finishing high school." Those who have achieved social status or who possess financial wealth, power, or fame naturally tend to assume that they are somehow better than others.

But arrogance is not just a problem with the wealthy or the upper classes of society. I find it alive and active among the poor as well. I know people with very little who look down on their relatives and friends because they have not had the same religious experience or because they lack a certain skill or ability. Arrogance is the fruit borne of a heart shaped by pride; in many ways, arrogance is the native language of our selfish hearts.

Arrogance in the life of a Christian reveals that we have failed to truly understand the gospel of God's grace. For example, I have some Muslim neighbors, and I can honestly say that they have been better neighbors to me and my wife than we have been to them. Being a Christian should not lead me to assume that I am somehow superior to others in any way. It should not surprise us to find non-Christians who do a better job of raising their kids or who excel in other moral virtues. The gospel, while transforming my life, does not somehow make me superior to others; if anything, it reminds me that I am no better than anyone else apart from God's grace.

Paul is aware of the danger of arrogance and its ability to undermine the radical nature of Christian love, so he draws attention to it as a potential problem in the church of Corinth. Immediately after telling us that "love does not ... boast," Paul goes on to tell us that love "is not arrogant" (1 Cor. 13:4d). The verb translated "arrogant" (ESV) or "proud" (NIV) literally means "to puff up." It conveys the idea of being "inflated" or being "full of one's own importance."[1] This verb is used only seven times in the New Testament, six of which are in 1 Corinthians.[2] Based on the frequency of the word in this letter, it would seem that arrogance was a real problem for the Corinthian church.

In 1 Corinthians 8:1, Paul uses this verb and writes that there is a form of knowledge that "puffs up," but it is not the kind of knowledge that accords with the radical love we see in the gospel. Love, Paul says, "builds up." It seeks the good of others and is not interested in comparisons to them or advantages to be gained. Christian love cares little for self-exaltation because it is focused on Christ and on sharing the love of Christ with others.

UNDERSTANDING TRUE GREATNESS

William Carey (1761–1834) is often called "the father of modern missions," and he was one of the greatest linguists the world has ever seen. In addition to translating the Bible into the (Indian) Bengali language by himself, "he supervised and edited translations of the Scriptures into thirty-six [Indian] languages; produced a massive Bengali-English dictionary, pioneered social reform, and founded the Agricultural and Horticultural Society of India."[3] Carey led an accomplished life by any worldly standards, yet he never forgot that he got his start in life as a cobbler, mending shoes.

William Barclay describes an incident from his life: "When he came to India, he was regarded with dislike and contempt. At a dinner party, a snob, with the idea of humiliating him, said in a tone that everyone could hear: 'I suppose, Mr. Carey, you once worked as a shoemaker.' 'No, your lordship,' answered Carey, 'not a shoemaker, only a cobbler.'"[4] As Barclay says, "He did not even claim to make shoes—only to mend them." This man was one genius who did not suffer from pride!

Jesus overturned common ideas of true greatness through the circumstances of his life. He was not born into a privileged family. At the time of his birth, no concessions seem to have been made for his parents, Mary and Joseph. Jesus was laid in a manger (Luke 2:7), a simple animal feeding trough, and when he was brought to the temple for his purification, his parents offered the best they could, "a pair of turtledoves, or two young pigeons" (Luke 2:24)—a concession made for those who could not afford the usual sacrifice of a lamb (Lev. 12:6–8).

Shortly after his birth, Jesus was taken to Egypt as a refugee. When he returned to Israel, he grew up in Nazareth, one of the smallest towns in the Galilee region (John 1:46). The rumor that Jesus was an "illegitimate" child may even have been the subject of gossip as he was growing up in Nazareth. Historically, we know that the story that Jesus' father was a Roman soldier billeted in Nazareth was a common Jewish polemic against Christianity from at least the middle of the second century.[5]

Since Joseph does not appear alongside Mary in the gospel narratives of Jesus' ministry and he is most commonly known as "Mary's son" (Mark 6:3), we can surmise that Joseph is likely to have died when Jesus was in his late teens or early twenties. As the eldest son, Jesus would have been responsible for managing the family carpentry business. British New Testament scholar R. T. France points out: "With at least four younger brothers and an unknown number of sisters to be brought up [Mark 6:3], the hope of formal education beyond the normal level must have been remote." Therefore, "to the superior eyes of Jerusalem he was uneducated" (John 7:15).[6] Jesus spent the final three years of his life living on the road—essentially homeless (Matt. 8:20). On top of all this, he died an ignoble death on a cross, suffering great pain and shame.

Despite his lack of worldly advantages, Jesus was the greatest human being who has ever lived. Throughout history, those who are rich and poor, kings and peasants, educated and uneducated have paid homage to him, bending their knee and owning him as their Lord and Savior. By his life and example, Jesus demonstrates to us that *true greatness does not depend on the things we usually associate with success and status*—worldly advantages and achievements.

The apostle Paul tells us that at one time in his life he, too, looked at Jesus and considered him a nobody. But Paul goes on to tell us that the revelation of Christ in the gospel completely changed his perspective: "From now on [after Jesus died and rose again], therefore, we regard no one according to the flesh. Even though we once regarded Christ according to the flesh, we regard him thus no longer" (2 Cor. 5:16).

From a human perspective, Paul says, Jesus of Nazareth was nothing special. But having met Christ, Paul can no longer see people in the same way. He can only see them through the lens of the gospel. It no longer matters to Paul whether a person is high or low in the eyes of the world. What really matters is being a new creature in Christ (2 Cor. 5:17). If someone knows Christ, they are Paul's brother or sister. If they do not know Christ, Paul longs for their salvation.

To put it simply, the gospel changes the way we see other people.

THE PEARL OF GREAT PRICE

Consider the following scenario. There are two brothers. One brother is "rich" relative to the other, with a net worth of $200,000 compared to the $20,000 net worth of his "poor" brother. Because one brother is ten times richer than the other, the wealthier brother considers himself upper class and avoids contact with his poorer brother. He believes that his money gives him an elevated social status, and he refuses to socialize with him.

One day, however, a wealthy, unmarried uncle of the two brothers dies and leaves each of them $600 million as an inheritance. What each brother formerly possessed is insignificant in comparison to their newfound wealth. The formerly "rich" brother can no longer claim to be richer than his brother.

Something similar occurs when we receive God's salvation. Jesus compares entering into God's kingdom with purchasing a pearl of great price. A person would be willing to sell all his possessions just to get that pearl, it was so highly valued (Matt. 13:46). In comparison to the incomparable riches we receive in Christ, all other worldly status symbols vanish into insignificance.

And yet our riches in Christ do not make us proud, for *we realize that we do not deserve anything that we have received.* We know we have been elevated to a high position, as princes and princesses in the kingdom of the Lord of lords and the King of kings. This knowledge should not puff us up with pride; it should be a source of joy and gratitude. Gratitude focuses us on another, whereas arrogance and pride focus on self. In gratitude, we know that all our riches are gifts given to us by our gracious God. We remember that we do not *deserve* any of the exalted status we have been given by God. The experience of grace thrills us because of our exalted identity in Christ, and at the same time it keeps us humble. The success and the gifts of others are not a threat to us because we are secure in Christ. We no longer have a need to make people feel inferior to us. Instead, out of the strength of our exalted identity in Christ, we can devote ourselves to serving others and lifting them up.

Love leads to servanthood, not arrogance.

STRENGTH FOR SERVANTHOOD

Arrogant people cannot be servants. Neither can people who do not have a secure sense of identity. Some of the people we describe as humble and as exhibiting the quality of servanthood are actually angry people—angry about the way people are exploiting them. This anger comes out when they are provoked enough to reveal something of their inner feelings. Often what flows out is a torrent of bitterness. It takes strength to be a servant of people. The identity that comes through the experience of grace gives us that strength.

There are three popular passages that describe the servanthood of Jesus, each of which begins with an affirmation of Christ's exalted identity. Mark 10:45 says, "For even the Son of Man came not to be served but to serve, and to give his life as a ransom for many." Deriving from prophecies in Daniel 7, "the phrase ['The Son of Man'] came to be used as a title of dignity for Jesus."[7] The text says that this "Son of Man *came*," which implies that he came from God. So this verse begins with an affirmation of the greatness of Christ, and then goes on to describe his mission as a servant.

John 13:3–15 records the incident of Christ washing the feet of the disciples. It begins with the statement: "Jesus, knowing that the Father had given all things into his hands, and that he had come from God and was going back to God, rose from supper. He laid aside his outer garment, and taking a towel …" (John 13:3–4). Again, note the statement of the exalted identity of Christ followed by a description of his act of servanthood.

Philippians 2:5–11 is the third passage, which describes how Jesus "emptied himself, by taking the form of a servant … he humbled himself" (2:7). But before that, we are told that Jesus, "though he was in the form of God, did not count equality with God a thing to be grasped" (2:6). Exalted identity, followed by genuine humility.

In the same vein, it is our exalted identity in Christ that gives us the strength to be humble servants. We don't need to show that we are great people, because we know that God has lifted us up to a great position as his beloved children. Now we can give ourselves to lifting up others. As a new Christian Paul experienced this lifting up when Barnabas took him to the apostles at a time that they were afraid of him, and he told them Paul's story (Acts 9:26–27). This act showed Paul features of the upside-down kingdom of God, where the senior person acts as a public relations officer of the junior person.

Paul himself followed in the steps of Barnabas in lifting others. He often went into raptures thinking about how God had exalted him through his grace (e.g., 1 Tim. 1:11–17). This grace gave him a motivation to lift others up in keeping with his advice: "Outdo one another in showing honor" (Rom. 12:10). So he names junior people like Silvanus and Timothy as co-authors of his letters (Phil. 1:1; Col. 1:1; 1 Thess. 1:1; 2 Thess 1:1; Philem. 1:1). We find him giving glowing tributes about his colleagues Timothy and Titus (2 Cor. 8:16–24; Phil. 2:19–24). In the last chapter of his most theological book, Romans, thirty-four mostly unknown people are named, with commendations about some of them and greetings to or from others.

Lifting up others is a thing that great people do! My first experience of speaking at a major international conference was at Amsterdam 83, a conference for itinerant evangelists convened by Billy Graham. I was thirty-five years old at the time, and I spoke on the evangelist's role in raising up younger evangelists. One of the things I said was that evangelists could take younger people with them when they go out to preach so that they could learn about this ministry. Dr Graham was not in the audience when I spoke, but he had watched my talk live on television in a room near to the auditorium. After I had finished speaking, he came up to the platform and spoke to me. Sadly, there was no one I knew who could take a photograph of this encounter! After thanking me for my message, he told me that he would like to travel with me when I go preaching in Asia, so that he could learn how to preach to Asians! A great man lifting up an unknown young preacher!

BEWARE! PRIDE GOES BEFORE A FALL

The Bible warns us about the dangers of arrogance when it says, "Pride goes before destruction, and a haughty spirit before a fall" (Prov. 16:18). Pride can be terribly destructive; yet Christians remain safe and secure when they trust God's grace to do for them what they cannot do by themselves. Peter describes believers as those "who by God's power are being *guarded through faith* for a salvation ready to be revealed in the last time" (1 Pet. 1:5, emphasis mine). Pride is dangerous because it leads us to think that our own abilities are sufficient, rather than learning to depend on God. Paradoxically, we are weakest when we feel strong (in ourselves) and strongest when we are weak (and dependent on the Lord). Paul warns us of this danger, inherent in pride: "Let anyone who thinks that he stands take heed lest he fall" (1 Cor. 10:12).

In our work with drug dependents we have found that recovering addicts often experience this in painful ways. It is not uncommon for a recovering addict to become judgmental at some point during the course of recovery. It is typically an early step in the process that leads to a major fall back into their addiction. A man becomes proud of his achievement, having kicked the habit, and he now looks at other Christians as hypocrites. This attitude of arrogance is not a sign of strength, however. It is a sign of someone trusting in his own strength rather than the strength that comes from God's grace. Grace is what gives a person the strength to overcome sin. Now without grace, he is vulnerable to a big fall.

The judgmental attitude that accompanies arrogance is also dangerous. Jesus said, "Judge not, that you be not judged" (Matt. 7:1). The use of what is called the present imperative in the Greek suggests a habit, an easy trap to fall into, of condemning other people. When Jesus says "that you be not judged," he may be saying that those who are judgmental could end up doing worse things than the things they are condemning. Sadly, this happens often. Some people who harshly condemn sexual sin in the church end up committing serious sexual sins themselves. The phrase "that you be not judged" could also mean that God will judge us for taking his place and judging people, which is one of his tasks. When people become arrogant and judgmental, it indicates that something dangerous is going on in their lives. Let us learn to fear arrogance!

, , ,

Pride, far from being a sign of strength, is actually a sign of our weakness. When we have a strong sense of the security, identity, and joy that grace brings, we are able to reach out to others in love and are empowered to lift them up instead of serving ourselves. But when we lack this strength, we feel insecure. We tend to look at others as our rivals or we want to show that they are lower than us. We try to project an image of being significant people.

When we encounter pride in another person, we should view it through the eyes of grace. Otherwise we may get so upset with the person that we may act or think in ways that are unhelpful to us and to that person. The vision of grace makes us have compassion for the arrogant person and helps us to react to arrogance constructively and lovingly. In this way we can minimize the damage the arrogant person causes without unnecessarily hurting ourselves and others. So not only is love not arrogant; it responds to arrogance with a humility that can help change an arrogant person.

CHAPTER 12

SENSITIVITY TO OTHERS

1 CORINTHIANS 13:5A

J. B. LIGHTFOOT (1828–1889) was an eminent New Testament scholar at Cambridge University, who was able to present learned and faithful biblical scholarship at a time when attacks on the trustworthiness of the Scriptures were growing. He later became Bishop of Durham. He said of Arthur F. Sim, one of his students: "Let him go where he will; his face will be a sermon in itself." William Barclay, who cites this, writes: "There is a graciousness in Christian love which never forgets that courtesy and tact and politeness are lovely things."[1] Loving people are sensitive to the feelings of others and to the things they value. Christians should seek to show their love for other people by demonstrating sensitivity and graciousness, especially in the midst of disagreement and conflict. One of the most visible marks of Christian love is that it avoids rudeness—behavior, words, and attitudes that communicate a lack of grace.

WHAT IS RUDENESS?

Translators have sought to communicate Paul's words in 1 Corinthians 13:5 in a variety of ways. The ESV renders this verse: "Love ... is not ...

rude." The NIV 2011 comes closer to the original meaning with the rendering, "Love ... does not dishonor others." Gordon Fee, in his commentary on 1 Corinthians, points to the merits of the rendering in the King James Version: love "doth not behave itself unseemly."[2] The Greek verb used here (aschēmoneō) characterizes action and words that are "in defiance of social and moral standards, with resulting disgrace, embarrassment, and shame."[3] Literally, the word here means "what is not according to proper form." In other words, unseemly behavior is behavior that fails to communicate honor and respect to others and is not sensitive to their feelings and scruples.

The notion of unseemly behavior or rudeness depends on the idea of shame. In most non-Western cultures, what is right and what is wrong is determined by whether an action brings honor or shame to a person. In recent years this notion of shame has become more important in the West as well.[4] The Bible frequently presents certain actions as shameful or unseemly, and that can serve as a deterrent to doing them. Given the importance of shame in all cultures, we should seek to avoid unnecessarily causing someone else to be put to shame by our actions.

When I was returning from a visit to one of our centers, a colleague asked me to carry a message to a home in a village that I would pass by where Youth for Christ was ministering. This was in the days before we had mobile phones, so it meant that I had to personally travel to the house to relay the message. I remember that I was busy that day and I had a meeting I had to attend later in my hometown of Colombo, so I hoped to deliver the message and then leave quickly afterward.

After delivering the message, the people at the home asked me to stay a bit longer and join them for a cup of tea. Knowing that I didn't have time to stay, I told them I was in a hurry and asked them to please excuse me. Several days later I learned that there was some talk around town about the Youth for Christ Director (me) who had come to the village but was too proud to have a cup of tea in a poor villager's home. Too late, I learned an important lesson about communicating love in the context of this culture: *if I cannot stay for a cup of tea, I should not go there at all.*

To serve people with love, we must be willing to give up whatever habits or preferences we have that unnecessarily offend them, and we must be willing to act in ways that make us uncomfortable. Some people pride themselves in their honesty, their willingness to be frank with others. Others are proud of their spontaneity. They like to do what they want, when they want. And there is nothing *necessarily* wrong with speaking honestly and being spontaneous. At times, these character qualities can be refreshing and helpful. But they can also be offensive to people and unnecessarily turn them off, so that we forfeit an opportunity to serve them.

In 1 Corinthians, Paul gives us three examples of the type of behavior he has in mind. In 1 Corinthians 7:36, Paul says that it is "rude" (*aschēmoneō*) when a man chooses not to marry his fiancée, after having made her wait for a long time, saying that God has called him to be single. In first-century culture, and in many places around the world today (including my native Sri Lanka), this would have been a disaster for the woman. The principle we can learn from this example is that *we must be careful when making promises of commitment.* If we break our promise to someone because it seems inconvenient to us, it can harm that person. Unless we have promised to do something that is clearly wrong or would force us to compromise our commitment to Christ, we may need to do some things we do not like to do in order to be faithful to our promises. Given that marriage is a commitment we make for the rest of our lives, we should exercise wisdom and be careful not to marry the wrong person. Paul's statement implies that we must be careful when we make promises to another person if there is a possibility that we will not be able to fulfill them.

The second example of "rudeness" occurs in 1 Corinthians 11:2–16, where women are asked to cover up their heads during worship. David Gill provides some cultural background, explaining that the covering of the head "became an emblem for modesty and chastity. Presumably women who felt able to uncover their heads were considered immodest, unchaste, and therefore by definition un-Roman."[5] Obviously, this is not true in most cultures today. While some Christian traditions have adopted the idea that women should cover their heads in worship (and it seems to me to be a beautiful way to honor God), it is difficult to insist on biblical grounds that women must always cover their heads. Paul is applying a principle here, showing how the virtue of modesty can be expressed by women in the context of Roman culture.

Though the application of the principle may vary from culture to culture, the basic principle of being decently attired for worship still applies, and this is where we must be careful to exercise our Christian freedom in ways that show love and respect for others. In the Roman Catholic Church near our home, there is a season of weddings every year from May to July. One year the church displayed a notice during this time regarding proper attire. It let people know that the church would do all it could to provide meaningful weddings for those who were getting married, and it requested people to dress modestly so that God would be honored during the service. If some women wore clothes that were too short or exposed too much, the notice said that the church could provide small scarves and sheets to those attending, to cover their exposed bodies. In Sri Lanka, where there is a cultural value of modesty in dress, many non-Christians find the way Christians dress for church to be "irreverent"—a stumbling block to serious consideration of the Christian religion.

Again, the basic principle is that *we dress in such a way as to communicate respect for God.* Sometimes an extravagant dress becomes a distraction to those attending a service. Many years ago we held an evangelistic rally in our church, a faith community consisting mainly of poor people with limited financial resources. I remember seeing one of the people who lives in our neighborhood come in for the meeting, only to leave a few minutes later, before everything started. When a member of our church stopped him to ask why he was leaving, he told him that his clothes were not good enough for him to attend our church. Following that incident, my wife and I made an intentional decision that we would not dress in a way that would make the poor in our community feel unwelcome in our church.

In addition to exercising wisdom in making commitments and promises and showing respect for the values of a culture in which we minister, Paul gives us a third principle in 1 Corinthians 11:17–34. Here Paul reports on a conflict in the church at Corinth because those who were wealthy were eating the food for the church's celebration of the Lord's Supper, leaving nothing for the poor. One group in the church was *choosing to fulfill their desires without considering the needs of others.* We can be guilty of this as well, in many different ways, but at the root of our "rudeness" is selfishness, a lack of consideration for others.

The habit of not being considerate about the needs of others and thinking only of our own needs is often seen in marriages. A husband convenes a meeting at his home, and his wife gets the house ready for it. After the meeting is over, the husband goes to his room and watches TV while his wife has to do all the clean-up. The husband is being rude to his wife because he has selfishly exploited her.

GRACELESS CONVERSATION

Like many other sins, unseemliness is expressed often in the way we talk. Paul has something to say about this in Colossians 4:6: "Let your speech ['conversation,' NIV] always be gracious, seasoned with salt, so that you may know how you ought to answer each person." Graced people are "gracious" in the way they talk. We see a lot of rudeness today because people live with a general sense of annoyance. I sense this attitude in comments such as these: "Life is not good"; "People are inconsiderate"; "No one really thinks about my welfare"; "I can't be thinking of and waiting for others to go forward with what I need to do." This can trigger actions indicating annoyance, like loud horn blowing on the road or rude talking on the phone.

Graced people also face unkindness, but their dominant emotion is joy coming out of thanksgiving to the Lord, who has done so much for them by showering his abundant grace on them. Grace gives us the strength to lift up people without pulling them down. We are affirming in the way we talk to people. This kind of behavior comes from regarding people with respect. It is said that when Nelson Mandela was President of South Africa, people were impressed by his deferential treatment of everyone he met. His aids would chastise him for rising from his chair to greet everyone who approached him.[6]

There is a common scenario that takes place in Sri Lanka that applies to other countries as well. Here is a young woman who is at an age when she could get married. She has not found someone suitable and possibly will not find someone for many years. God may even have called her to be single. But wherever she goes people ask her, "Any good news?" meaning, of course, good news about prospects of marriage. This becomes a huge burden as she is not happy when people highlight her singleness in this way.

Finally, she does get married, but she does not have a child for many years. Again she is bombarded with the question, "Any good news?" this time referring to her having a baby. Then a child is born. Four years later, another child is born. Now people tell the elder child things like, "Now your parents will have to look after your sister, and they won't have time for you." I have really heard this statement said to a little child! Such statements add to the insecurity that has arisen from a complete change in the way this child's home had been run during the first four years of his life.

People say such insensitive things without thinking about the consequences of their words. It is evidence that they do not respect the person enough to ask what the consequences or their words are. That is a form of rudeness!

Parents of the young people we work with sometimes tell me that these youth may have a strong commitment to service within our ministry but that they speak rudely to their parents at home and often say hurtful things. This can be said about fathers and mothers too. Sometimes I know a person is speaking to his wife on a cell phone because the tone used in speaking is much less warm and friendly than when someone else calls. True, within a ministry people have spiritual responsibilities that necessitate that they be on their best behavior. When they come home, their guard is dropped and they can be their true selves.

But for Christians, being your true self involves being kind to loved ones. We said in the Introduction that agape love is decisive. It decides to do what is not natural. As a result, we ought to make a decision to stop the words of annoyance that come up almost naturally and use God's strength to enable us to speak kindly to our loved ones. God will honor such decisions. People who work hard at their jobs and ministry need to work hard at their home life too.

Don't worry; this won't leave you exhausted. Showing love to family members is a richly rewarding activity. Though our surface reaction to family members can be one of annoyance, deep down we desire to love them. When we make the effort to show kindness to them, we feel good inside and experience God's peace—or shalom. We have become what we are made to be. There is a deep satisfaction in that.

If we feel under a lot of pressure and ready to snap sometimes, we can tell our family members that we are facing a difficult situation and to excuse us if we snap unreasonably. They want deep down to think good thoughts about us. They will appreciate our willingness to be vulnerable with them, and they may end up doing what they can to help reduce our pressure. There is a remarkable freedom that comes to a home where people are not afraid to share their weaknesses and problems.

Another key to help us overcome the irritability that comes with pressure is spending time with God. When we are close to God, the security of his eternity rubs off on us and we develop security within ourselves, which results in a reduction of pressure. Psalm 46:10 says, "Be still, and know that I am God. I will be exalted among the nations, I will be exalted in the earth!" Isaiah 26:3–4 says, "You keep him in perfect peace whose mind is stayed on you, because he trusts in you. Trust in the LORD forever, for the LORD GOD is an everlasting Rock." When we spend time with God, the security that belongs to our everlasting, almighty rock comes into us as well. We slow down from the rushed attitude that binds our lives by rooting our attitudes on eternity. That, in turn, takes away the irritability that can control our behavior.

I have heard a helpful story about a Christian woman who has been identified as Susannah Wesley in several websites, though I am not certain about that.[7] This woman had many children (Susannah had nineteen, of whom nine died as infants). A neighbor would help her when she was very busy. The neighbor once told the woman that she was so surprised at how much at peace and close to God she seemed to be even though she had so many children. She asked her for her secret. The mother pointed to a large apron she was wearing. She said that there was a rule in the house that when mother put her apron over her head and sat on a special chair at home, she was praying and must not be disturbed. The children learned to keep the rule, and the mother went to pray whenever she felt the pressure was getting too much. Through contact with God, her nerves were relaxed by the security of being under almightiness. Prayer can be a great antidote to rudeness!

UNINTERESTING CONVERSATION

Paul's teaching in Colossians 4:6 not only presents graciousness as a feature of Christian conversation, but it also instructs us that our conversation should be "seasoned with salt." Commentator Peter O'Brien explains that this means that the conversation "must not be dull or insipid but should be interesting and [the words] judiciously chosen."[8]

I sometimes find myself pleading with God to get someone to stop speaking as he or she rambles on about a matter of little concern or interest. Over the years, I have come to accept this as a calling from God, to give lonely people a listening ear. But this does not excuse people from being sensitive to others when they talk. Love is expressed by choosing our words wisely, making sure we do not monopolize a conversation or take advantage of a listening ear.

Sometimes our conversation is inappropriate, not because it is overtly rude, but simply because it is too complicated and elaborate for the time and place. A girl asked her mother, "What makes the moon white?" The mother replied, "I do not know. Why don't you ask your father?" She said, "Oh, I don't want to know that much about it!" His explanations were inappropriate because they were too elaborate.

After an operation I needed to take my wife for some important follow up visits to the doctor every few days. On one of these occasions, I had dropped my wife off at the entrance of the hospital and had gone to park the car. While I was rushing back to the office to catch up with her, I met a dear Christian brother who went on excitedly testifying about God's goodness to him. I confess that I did not know how to stop him from talking. Thankfully, someone came by and released me from listening by stopping by to say, "Hello." The break provided by that person gave me an opportunity to explain that my wife was waiting for me. When I finally caught up with her, I learned that the procedure had been completed and she was waiting for me to come in so that she could pay the bill!

, , ,

Love is sensitive to others in simple but significant ways. Love desires the best for them, so we are careful to find ways to speak and act so that they will be edified. A loving person learns to become sensitized to cultural and personal factors that affect others and always seeks the best for people. This may mean that we will often be inconvenienced because of others, but for a Christian that is not a major problem because, as the next chapter shows, love "does not insist on its own way."

CHAPTER 13

VICTORY THROUGH SURRENDER

1 CORINTHIANS 13:5B

SURRENDER! IT'S A WORD that is often seen as negative. It communicates the idea that we have been defeated, that we have lost the battle. Yet for a Christian, *surrender* is a glorious term. Stanley Jones, an American missionary and an effective evangelist to intellectuals in South Asia, popularized this idea of *Victory through Surrender* in a book he wrote by that name.[1] Jones taught that there are different ways that we can respond to the fact that we have been tainted by sin and now live in a world corrupted by the influence of sin. Some choose to indulge themselves and do whatever they want. Others deny their desires and choose the path of asceticism. The Christian way, however, is to surrender the self to God. God redeems it in Christ and gives it back to us to live according to the plan he had for us when he created us. Surrender of the self is the only way to be truly human because it helps us align ourselves with the purpose of our Creator.

In 1 Corinthians 13:5, Paul presents another aspect of radical love to us: "[Love] does not insist on its own way." If we don't understand this characteristic of love from the perspective of victory through surrender, it will appear as a dreary duty that contradicts the freedom and vibrancy of the abundant life Christ offers to his followers. Paul is not prescribing a life of deprivation but pointing to the path toward true liberation.

SURRENDER IN A SELFISH WORLD

In 1 Corinthians 8 Paul talks about showing love by seeking the good of others, even if it means sacrificing your own freedom as a Christian. Paul encouraged those in Corinth who were "stronger" Christians, who did not struggle with eating meat sacrificed to idols, to be willing to give up what they were doing (eating meat) so as not to be a stumbling block to their "weaker" brothers and sisters in faith. Then, in chapter 9, Paul offers himself as an example of this principle, describing how he willingly chose to become a slave, serving the needs of others and not his own good, in order to bring the gospel to them.

Paul follows this in the next chapter with an encouragement that the Corinthian Christians should also act in this way: "Let no one seek his own good, but the good of his neighbor" (1 Cor 10:24). Again, Paul uses his own life as an example of what he is asking of the Corinthians — he himself practices what he is preaching: " ... just as I try to please everyone in everything I do, not seeking my own advantage, but that of many, that they may be saved" (10:33).

In his letter to the Philippian church, Paul offers a similar challenge, stressing that unselfish love and the surrender of our own good for the sake of others is the key to maintaining unity and fellowship in the church: "Let each of you look not only to his own interests, but also to the interests of others" (Phil. 2:4). Sadly, we live in a world where selfishness has become respectable. There is much emphasis today on finding your own self-worth and living out your full potential, but this common understanding of "self-worth" is very different from the biblical understanding of our value as people made in the image of God.

Along with this comes the rise of individualism and decline of long-term commitments. In our fast-moving global culture, people change locations, jobs, churches, and spouses in rapid succession. The idea that we should sacrifice our plans, our desires, our goals in life for the sake of others seems a waste of time. It looks inefficient, and we question, if God wants us to be productive, why he would ever call us to such a lifestyle. The lifestyle of loving Christian service for the good of others is challenging to live out today because most people will think we are failures if we decide to give up our personal plans and dreams for the sake of others.

Wants have now become rights, and there is a pervasive sense that we "deserve" certain things that used to be considered luxuries reserved only for a few people. A bank in Sri Lanka now advertises "lifestyle loans" to purchase nonessential luxuries. They advertise with the slogan: Don't ask "Why?" — ask "Why *not*?" This kind of thinking, when we live and breathe it every day, fosters a mind-set of entitlement and inhibits people from being willing to forego things they want for the sake of others.

True greatness — the kind of greatness borne of a radical call to love others — is not borne through a sense of entitlement. Many of the satisfactions and achievements that people seek today are nothing more than shallow, temporary gains. They are not the rewards of lifelong commitment and faithfulness. And the pursuit of such a life is a sure source of dissatisfaction. Stanley Jones says it this way:

> If you don't surrender to God don't think you don't surrender. Everybody surrenders to something. Some surrender to themselves as God. If you surrender to yourself as God you won't like your God. You will do as you like and then you won't like what you do. You will express yourself and you won't like the self you express. You won't like yourself and no one else will like you.[2]

Jones reminds us that we all end up serving something or someone in life. Those who seek to please themselves end up serving their desires, and the fruit they bear is not all that attractive. When we seek to please God, we serve his desires, and the fruit we bear lasts forever.

Surrendering to God means believing that God knows what is best for us. Our wisdom is far below God's wisdom (see Isa. 55:8–9). Therefore, we gladly ask God each day, "What do you want me to crucify today?" Far from a morbid desire to sacrifice or seek our own unhappiness, we give up our selfish desires because we are driven by a burning passion for the best in life. As we surrender our plans to God, we are encouraged by the promise of Jesus, "For whoever would save his life will lose it, but whoever loses his life for my sake and the gospel's will save it" (Mark 8:35).

As I was preparing to step down from my position as National Director of Youth for Christ in Sri Lanka after serving in that role for thirty-five years, I had some time to reflect on my time of service. One of the things I realized was that over the course of those thirty-five years, I repeatedly had to give up many of my plans, ambitions, and opportunities in order to attend to needs within the ministry of Youth for Christ and within the nation of Sri Lanka. The relief operations after the great tsunami of 2004 forced me to give up a writing sabbatical. When I was finally able to take this sabbatical, I could not write as I had wanted to because there was a need to raise funds for the studies of our staff. So, instead of writing, I taught in seminaries abroad to earn money for the staff.

Yet as I look back on these years, I now see that almost all of my dreams have been fulfilled; some of them just took several years longer than I had planned. In the end, the delay undoubtedly made the end product better than anything I could have achieved if I followed my original plans. I can try hard to feel sorry for myself, but it doesn't work—the inescapable truth is that God has richly blessed me!

When you know you are following God's ways, there is a sense of joy and peace that make any sacrifices well worth it. Joy and peace are the greatest earthly treasures one can have. And the cause for this joy and peace is our love relationship with the Lord Jesus, who is our Savior, Friend, Brother, and Lord. We know that this relationship cannot be broken, regardless of what happens to us along the path of service.

In fact, Paul presents this conviction in vivid style in Romans 8:35–39. He begins: "Who shall separate us from the love of Christ? Shall tribulation, or distress, or persecution, or famine, or nakedness, or danger, or sword?" (8:35). Paul goes on to talk about the cost he has paid to serve God: "As it is written, 'For your sake we are being killed all the day long; we are regarded as sheep to be slaughtered'" (8:36). He next testifies that suffering for the cause of Christ, giving up his worldly ambitions, is not a sign of his defeat: "No, in all these things we are *more than conquerors* through him who loved us" (8:37, emphasis added). Finally, Paul exults once more in the deepest reality in our life, our love relationships with God: "For I am sure that neither death nor life, nor angels nor rulers, nor things present nor things to come, nor powers, nor height nor depth, nor anything else in all creation, will be able to separate us from the love of God in Christ Jesus our Lord" (8:38–39).

The love of God for us in Christ is the deepest reality we can know. With such riches in Christ, we gladly give up anything, if that is what God asks of us.

NO AMBITIONS?

At this point, you might wonder: Is it wrong to have personal ambition? Is it wrong to be driven to succeed?

Serving others with sacrificial love does not negate all ambition in life; rather, it transforms it into something different. Because we have fallen in love with God and have had glimpses of his glory, we now realize that we have the *honor* of reflecting his glory to others, here on earth (1 Cor. 10:31). We are not driven by selfish ambition, but by a burning ambition to glorify God in all that we do on earth.

We are committed to this and are willing to pay the price of excellence for the glory of God. We study and prepare meticulously; we work hard at what we do. In the Bible, the noun *kopos* and the verb *kopiaō* carry the idea of working hard to the point of exhaustion. Paul uses these two words ten and fourteen times respectively when he refers to the work that he and other Christians do for God (e.g., Col. 1:29; 1 Cor. 15:10, 58). So working hard is a key Christian value.

Christians are still driven people, but we are no longer driven by unfulfilling earthly ambition. Francis Xavier (1506–1552) was a Spanish Jesuit missionary in India and Japan who is credited to have been responsible for the conversion of 700,000 people to Christianity. He once sent a challenge to Europe: "Tell the students to give up their small ambitions and come eastward to preach the gospel of Christ." I like the way Xavier says that. Compared to the call of God to serve the lost with the love and message of the gospel, the ambitions we give up are really *small* ambitions. This attitude of surrender frees us to pursue our consuming passion for the great work of bringing glory to God.

SURRENDER AT WORK

Before we end this chapter, I want to look at some concrete examples of the type of surrender I am talking about.

The first example that comes to mind is a negative one we should avoid. Powerful Christian leaders will sometimes believe they have the freedom to do whatever they want because people view them as representatives of God and people are fearful of displeasing God by contradicting their leaders. In other words, their authority serves as a cover for doing what they think is right, and it inhibits accountability. What sometimes passes as ambition for the honor of God, when cloaked in an attitude of faith that rubber stamps risky ventures, is actually nothing more than the selfish ambition of leaders who want to build their own kingdoms.

Such kingdoms eventually crash and bring great dishonor to God. This is why it is important to ensure that every Christian leader is personally accountable to other people who can speak honestly into their life and confront unhealthy attitudes and behaviors. At the same time, it is necessary for those who serve these leaders to burn with a passion for the kingdom of God. Few things discourage a passionate leader as much as a board or committee filled with people who want to be careful (which is good) but have no real passion to see God glorified (which stifles progress). Good committee members will burn with zeal for God and his work but will love their leader enough to question him when they sense that he is acting in an unhealthy or unbiblical way.

Consider another example. A group of people is working on a major project together, and various members of the group are given responsibility for different aspects of the project. In the implementation of the plan, there may be more than one legitimate way to get the job done. In general, so long as it is does not break a law or violate a moral conviction, we should try to give people the freedom to do things the way they think is best, even though that may be different from the way we would have done it. Though we can share our opinion on the best way to do something, we should try to give the person responsible for the work the ability to do what he or she thinks is best.

Nevertheless, there may be times when it is best to give up our own desire for the sake of the community. For instance, people differ quite widely in their artistic tastes and opinions when it comes to interior design. If most of the people working on a project believe that a proposed color combination for a room is appropriate, we should not try to force our own tastes on the design. It is amazing to me how often Satan traps churches into battling over details like carpet and paint while there are lost people who need to hear the good news of Christ!

There are other people who look at every project as a battle for self-affirmation. I have encountered drivers who feel offended when someone passes them on the road. They battle through traffic to overtake the one who passed them, often driving dangerously—all for the sake of their offended honor.

I remember the difficulties we had when Youth for Christ was getting registered with the government. The secretary of our board, Chandran Williams, had done much of the preliminary work with the lawyers and the government officials. He was in business at the time and had far more experience than I did with these matters. Our lawyers presented our board with two options, two different ways of pursuing our registration. After hearing both options, Chandran ended up supporting one way while I supported the other.

There was much discussion and debate, but in the end the board decided to follow the way I had supported, and Chandran was a model of Christian love in submitting to the will of the board. Even though we had rejected his perspective, he supported the decision and was the one responsible for implementing the very suggestion he had argued against. As a volunteer, he could easily have stepped aside. But love does not insist on its own way. Love serves others and follows the leading of God by submitting to godly authority.

The biblical principle of not insisting on our own way is often violated when families divide an inheritance. A father gathered together his two children, a son and daughter, when he wanted to write his last will. He owned two houses, one a large and luxurious house and the other a small, run-down house. According to the common practice in the culture of that society, the son should have got the large house. But he was already wealthy, while his sister was poor since she had married an alcoholic who had squandered their wealth, and she was now widowed. The son insisted that the large house should go to his sister. Sadly, many supposedly Christian people forget their Christian principles when it comes to the dividing of family property. The result is hostile battles within families that bring great dishonor to God.

, , ,

When I was a student at Asbury Theological Seminary in the United States, I attended an out-of-town church for a weekend along with my fellow student Billy Kuartei (who later became a national leader in the Palauan islands in Micronesia). The understanding between us was that I would give a short testimony and he would preach on Sunday morning. Then, in the evening, he would share his testimony and I would preach.

Everything went according to plan in the morning. But in the evening, Billy shared a powerful testimony, and it was clear to everyone that God had moved among the people. I remember standing up to sing the song "How Great Thou Art," just before I was supposed to preach. As I was singing, I noticed that some people had begun to weep, and I realized that God had done the heart work he wanted to accomplish in this service, and that my job now was to help reap the harvest. So instead of preaching my prepared sermon, I gave some scriptural keys to guide people in responding to God, and I invited those who wanted to make a commitment to Christ to walk forward. Many people responded. I had to lay aside my desire to exhibit my preaching abilities to allow God to finish the work he had begun through Billy's sharing.

How foolish it is when we insist on our own way! Instead of pressing our rights and promoting what we believe we deserve, we should choose the path of surrender. Surrendering leads to true happiness, as we trust God, knowing that his way is so much better than our own.

CHAPTER 14

ANGER: THE VICE OF THE VIRTUOUS

1 CORINTHIANS 13:5C

THE SCOTTISH EVANGELIST, theologian, and scientist Henry Drummond (1851–1897) described anger as "the vice of the virtuous." He pointed out that those most prone to anger rarely see anger as a problem or a character flaw, much less a matter of sin. We tend to justify our anger, says Drummond, referring to it as a matter of temperament or personality, or a family trait; we certainly do not take it seriously as a vice. Yet in 1 Corinthians 13, Paul views anger as antithetical to radical love. As Drummond reminds us: "The Bible again and again returns to condemn [anger] as one of the most destructive elements of human nature."[1]

Paul tells us that "love ... is not irritable" (1 Cor. 13:5); that is, "it is not easily angered" (NIV). Paul is talking here about people who have a tendency to lose their tempers over the slightest provocation. Interestingly, Paul also discusses the issue of anger in his list of qualifications for leadership in the church, saying that an "overseer ... must not be ... quick-tempered" (Titus 1:7). Sometimes we appoint people to leadership in the church because they are talented or because they can motivate others to action effectively; yet in our zeal to find effective leaders, we may choose to ignore deeper character flaws like anger. Paul understood that leaders with quick tempers can do great harm to the name of Christ. They hurt those they lead through their unreasonable outbursts and can bring great dishonor to the cause of Christ if they publicly display their anger before the watching world.

RIGHTEOUS AND UNRIGHTEOUS ANGER

The anger Paul condemns here should be distinguished from what some have called "righteous anger." The expression "righteous anger" does not appear in the Bible, but the basic idea is present in statements like, "Be angry and do not sin" (Eph. 4:26). In several places the Bible seems to suggest that there is a way to express anger that is not sinful. We see this righteous anger expressed in the life of Jesus as he thunders against the hypocrites and the people who had turned the temple, the house of God, into a marketplace for buying and selling. Anger can also be seen as an expression of love, as when we see a person we care deeply about ruining his or her life through foolish and/or unrighteous living and we confront them with the truth. Another example of righteous anger can be found in Paul's letter to the Galatians, when he corrects them, using strong language after they were led astray by false teachers (Gal. 3:1–4).

Leon Morris points out: "It is a necessary part of moral character to abhor evil as well as to love good." God is actively opposed to evil, and as Morris writes: "Hundreds of biblical passages refer to the divine wrath. God is 'a God who expresses his wrath every day' (Ps. 7:11); 'our God is a consuming fire' (Heb. 12:29)." [2]

Since humans are made in the image of God, we need to express wrath in our lives too. But for most of us, the only "anger" we have experienced has been sinful and hurtful outbursts from ourselves or other fallible human beings, so we find it difficult to associate God's goodness with his wrath and anger. But we should remember that when the Bible speaks of God's wrath burning against our sin (e.g., Exod. 22:24; 32:10), it is not referring to a passing emotion motivated by a bruised ego. God's wrath is not an arbitrary response—it is his settled and just opposition to all that is wrong and evil in this world ... and the sin in our hearts. In fact, rather than speaking negatively of God's anger, the Bible speaks approvingly about the anger of God as an expression of his holiness and his commitment to uphold justice.

When the Bible speaks about human expressions of anger, however, it is more disapproving. The vast majority of instances of anger we see among humans *can* be categorized as sinful. They are not motivated by love for the person, nor are they rooted in authentic zeal for the glory of God. This is why refraining from responding to an offense out of anger can be so powerful. It's entirely unexpected in a world where retaliation is the norm.

In June 2011, Leonard Fernando (not a relative) succeeded me as the National Director of Youth for Christ (YFC) in Sri Lanka. About thirteen years prior, Leonard had moved to a predominantly non-Christian town to pioneer the ministry of YFC in that place. He erected a sign outside his house that announced that his home was now an office of YFC (a decision he later regretted and reversed). The sign was seen as offensive to many of the people who lived in the neighborhood, a challenge to other faiths.

Sometime around midnight, two weeks after moving to the village, a heavily intoxicated person began screaming obscenities outside Leonard's home. Making unfounded allegations, he threatened to set fire to the house unless the YFC sign was removed. Hearing the commotion, a crowd soon gathered outside his home. It was a terrifying experience for Leonard's young family. Thankfully, after continuing to shout and scream for some time, the man eventually left and the crowd dispersed.

The next morning Leonard decided that he would visit this man at his home. When Leonard arrived at the man's house, the man's wife was very happy to see him and she ran inside to announce his arrival to her husband. The man came out of his house and told Leonard that he had been unable to sleep that night. He shared that he had been deeply troubled by Leonard's response—or rather, Leonard's *lack* of a response. Even though the man had hurled obscenities, accusations, and threats at Leonard and his family, Leonard had kept a pleasant smile throughout the ordeal. Now, the man just could not get that smile out of his mind! It had troubled him so much that he could not fall asleep.

Leonard and the man continued to meet and talk in the days and weeks that followed, and they soon became good friends. When it came time, several years later, for Leonard to move to another house, his friend helped him find a place to live. There is power in choosing not to retaliate. By refusing to respond in anger, neither asserting his rights nor defending his honor, Leonard left a distinct impression on the man. By God's grace, his enemy became one of his friends. That's the power of the gospel.

If refusing to respond in anger is such a powerful witness to the gospel of God's grace in Jesus Christ, why is it that some people, even devout Christians, fly into a rage? In this and the next chapter I will explore five triggers to anger that I have encountered in my years of ministry. If we want to be known as people marked by radical love, we need to take each of these seriously and be prepared to respond appropriately.

1. CARELESSNESS: FAILING TO CONSIDER THE CONSEQUENCES

Anger can cause great damage in relationships and destroy our witness for God. This is why we must be extra careful in avoiding angry outbursts when we are provoked. Most often, anger is expressed through angry speech, though it can also take the form of physical violence. James describes some of the ravages caused by an uncontrolled tongue, vividly comparing the power of the tongue to the devastation caused by a wild fire (Jas. 3:5 – 6). I have personally experienced the damaging consequences that come when Christians fly into a rage, say terribly hurtful things to people, and then realize their error and try to make amends by apologizing to the hurt person.

Though the offending person may be able to move on and put it all behind them, these occasions leave wounds that take time to heal. A simple apology may not bring healing; sadly, the offended person may struggle with wounds for years to come. Jesus teaches that anger is serious, comparing it to the act of murder: "You have heard that it was said to those of old, 'You shall not murder, and whoever murders will be liable to judgment.' But I say to you that everyone who is angry with his brother [or sister] will be liable to judgment" (Matt. 5:21 – 22). Giving expression to our anger is dangerous, and we must be prepared to deal with the consequences.

To give an example: In the middle of an argument a daughter tells her mother, "Anyway, I am a burden on you, unlike my brother." The mother responds, "What made you think that? You know that's not true." The girl refers to an event seven years earlier when, in the height of an argument, the mother had made that statement. She never really meant it. In fact, many times the statements made by angry people do not really represent what they deeply believe. They say nasty things, ruled by their emotions or their pain at the moment, and don't realize how devastating those words can be to the other person. People need to know that what they say has the power to cause great damage.

In love, we must warn people when they speak to us or others like this. Aware of the dangers in confronting sin in others, Jesus outlined a procedure for dealing with personal offenses that involves going to a person who has hurt us. If that fails, we must take a witness along. If this, too, fails, Jesus instructs us to bring our concern before the local church leaders, who will work together to find a solution (Matt. 18:15–17). Why does Jesus give such elaborate instructions for dealing with offenses? *Because hurtful actions have significant consequences, and maintaining the unity of the church is vitally important.*

If someone continues to respond in anger, some discipline may be required to help heal that person's weakness. Forgiveness frees us from the guilt of sin, but discipline helps heal the weakness that caused us to sin. Two specific instances of discipline mentioned in Paul's letters describe the motivation for discipline as the healing and restoration of the sinner (1 Cor. 5:5; 1 Tim. 1:19–20). In these cases the discipline Paul recommended was severe (excommunication) because the sins committed were so serious (sexual relations with a step-mother and heresy), and the offenders were unrepentant. Depending on the severity of a person's anger, the discipline enforced to bring healing could, perhaps, take a milder form.

Consider a gifted worship leader who is prone to impatience with his wife and regularly scolds her with abusive language. He confesses his struggle to his friends, in keeping with the instruction in James 5:16: "Confess your sins to one another and pray for one another, that you may be healed." His friends ask him to report to them regularly on how he fares in this area. After several weeks, they learn that he continues to sin against his wife, and they let him know that if he does not change his behavior, he will be asked to refrain from leading worship for three months. Unfortunately, his behavior does not stop, and the church disciplines him as planned.

For the next three months he struggles when he goes to church for worship. The person who replaces him in leadership does not have the same gift to lead, and when he talks to people in the church, they tell him how much they hope he will be able to return and lead again. At the end of the three months he happily returns to his role as worship leader. Not long afterward, his wife does something that really annoys him again. As had been his practice before, the words well up in his mouth, ready to flow with devastating force. Then he remembers the painful three months under discipline. He checks his natural instinct and keeps quiet! The discipline has helped him to become serious about overcoming anger.

For many years after committing my life to Christ, despite the joy of a happy relationship with God, I found that I continued to struggle with a hot temper. Most of my anger was directed at my brothers and my mother, and I learned to regularly apologize for my outbursts. Sometimes I would try to pray at night before going to bed, and I would find that I could not come before God until I had first apologized to one of them. I remember waking my mother up from her sleep a few times just to do so! I believe that continuing to do this after my outbursts has helped me overcome this nasty habit, so that now this is not the problem it used to be.

There are always consequences to our anger. If we take a serious view of these consequences, we would be more careful about unreasonably flying into a rage. Accountability with other believers and the practice of church discipline can help us be more alert to the dangers of carelessness in expressing anger.

2. PRESSURE AND STRESS: OVERWORK, BUSYNESS, AND CHANGE

We tend to be tense when we face special pressures, and often this triggers angry outbursts. The pressure could be sickness or disharmony in the family, problems in the workplace, or financial difficulties. Or it can be due to an event like an upcoming presentation, a party we are responsible for planning, or a trip overseas.

One of the saddest, but all too common, examples of such outbursts of anger is in the family of an alcoholic or a drug addict. Because of the husband's irresponsibility, the wife has to work hard to make ends meet. She comes home from work tired and encounters abuse from her husband. But she does not give up working hard, so as to help her children and give them an opportunity to do well in life. Yet because of the strain in her life, she becomes irritable and tends to get unreasonably angry when her children do something that annoys her. She ends up hurting the children for whom she is sacrificing so much. This may be a scenario that happens in many homes, though perhaps in a less severe form. Ideally we should try to do everything we can to avoid putting ourselves in stressful situations. But some stress is inevitable. We cannot avoid our basic responsibilities and commitments, so we need to find a way of learning to cope with stress. I have used three proven strategies that have helped me to cope with stress in my life.

First, you must admit that you are experiencing stress. When Moses realized he had too many responsibilities, far more than he could handle alone, he talked to God about his problem, and his father-in-law Jethro helped him wisely delegate his responsibilities (see Exod. 18:13–26; Deut.

1:9–15). When my children were young, I remember experiencing some stressful situations at work. Knowing that I would be tempted to behave impatiently at home and take out some of my stress on my family, I made sure that my wife and children knew that I was under pressure, and I worked hard to apologize when I acted impatiently with them. By doing something concrete about the stress, we can get a handle on it and become sensitive to its adverse side effects. This sensitivity helps us avoid harmful outbursts.

Second, share your burdens with a friend. Paul said, "Bear one another's burdens, and so fulfill the law of Christ" (Gal. 6:2). Sharing with a trusted friend what is causing stress in your life may actually release some of the tension. Verbalizing a problem requires us to present it intelligently, and the effort we make to talk about it with another person may help us get a handle on our situation and respond constructively to it. Proverbs often instructs us to get advice from our friends (e.g., Prov. 12:15; 15:22; 19:20; 20:18). Ecclesiastes 4:9–10 says, "Two are better than one.... For if they fall, one will lift up his fellow. But woe to him who is alone when he falls and has not another to lift him up!" This is especially true when we find ourselves in stress-filled situations.

Third, hand over your burden to God. While the problem may seem huge, we must not forget that our greatest obstacles are nothing for the almighty God, who is sovereign over history. More often than not, God is ready to use the stress we face and turn our circumstances into an opportunity for his glory and goodness to be displayed in our lives. Most importantly, we must be reminded that God cares for us, his presence will sustain us, and he promises peace in response to our dependence on him.

Peter talks about "casting all your anxieties on him, because he cares for you" (1 Pet. 5:7). David says, "Cast your burden on the LORD, and he will sustain you" (Ps. 55:22). In a similar way, Paul tells us that we should come before God in an attitude of prayer and gratitude: "Do not be anxious about anything, but in everything by prayer and supplication with thanksgiving let your requests be made known to God" (Phil. 4:6). When we bring our concerns to God with this attitude, the promised reward is a peace that guards and protects us from the effects of stress. So Paul continues, "And the peace of God, which surpasses all understanding, will guard your hearts and your minds in Christ Jesus" (4:7). These three texts give three different results of casting our burdens on God. We experience God's *care*, his *sustenance*, and his *peace*.

About twenty years ago we had had a major crisis in our ministry, and I was at a loss to know how to move forward. We struggled for many weeks, and the final resolution took a long time to achieve. This was a very stressful time for me, and I got into the habit of spending nights alone with God. I would sit in my room at night talking to him, at times reading the Bible, and at times doing nothing but sitting. Even when I would sit alone, I was conscious that I was in the presence of God. These times of prolonged sitting with God helped calm my troubled soul and enabled me to face the stress in my life without outbursts of anger or despair. It was during this time that I also learned an important principle: *in a time of conflict, meet with God before you meet with people.* Our actions never spring simply as a reaction to what people do and say to us. They spring primarily from the call of God to be his servants and his sending us out to face the people we encounter in our ministry.

Of course, I could not stay up every night. I needed to sleep, but on some nights I found that I would struggle to sleep, tossing and turning in bed. Sleep eluded me during this time. During those nights I learned to consciously cast my problems on God. I would say to God: "I cannot handle this problem. I do not know what the answer is. But you know. So I place this burden upon you. Please help me to sleep." Almost always, I would fall asleep soon after that.

It goes without saying that when our lives are filled with stress, we must rely on God and spend time in his presence even more than normal. Sadly, that is exactly what we often do *not* do because we do not believe we have time for it. But we must make the time. We must let the truth of Deuteronomy 33:27 speak to our heart and mind: "The eternal God is your dwelling place, and underneath are the everlasting arms."

3. PHYSICAL WEAKNESS: LACK OF SLEEP, SICKNESS, AND POOR HEALTH

In addition to carelessness and stress, anger can be triggered because we are physically vulnerable and weak or tired. After Elijah had completed his grueling battle with the prophets of Baal on Mount Carmel, he found out that Jezebel wanted to kill him. He ran away, hid, and told God he wanted to die. Fear of Jezebel's anger seems to have triggered depression. But the fact that he was exhausted after his grueling spiritual battle with the prophets of Baal undoubtedly also contributed to the depression. We see evidence of this when God allowed Elijah to sleep for more than a day, waking him up only to feed him. God treated him much like a patient in a hospital, offering sleep and encouraging words as therapy for Elijah's fragile emotional state (see 1 Kings 18–19). There are times when we, too, need the rest and restoration that Elijah needed. Often, one of the most important things we can do when we are growing irritable is to rest and get adequate sleep.

I have found that irritability can be used by God to force me to reevaluate my schedule. The older I get, the more often I need to stop and cut things out from my schedule. Responsibilities have a way of accumulating, and before we realize it we are overloaded. Therefore, occasionally I try to stop and prune my schedule, sometimes cutting out some fairly serious responsibilities and commitments.

When a mother has to care for her little children, she is often physically exhausted. I advise husbands, who tend to be preoccupied by the supposedly more significant battles and stresses in their workplace, to take time to learn about the stress and the challenges their wives face and give them time to rest or enjoy some time away from the kids. Most husbands don't realize the extent of the pressure their wives are experiencing. Young mothers need time to be refreshed and to remember that their life and identity are not entirely defined by their responsibilities and roles as a mom. A loving husband will work to provide this for his wife by taking on some of her responsibilities or finding someone to care for the children for a while, to give his wife a break.

, , ,

Regardless of whether the source of our anger is carelessness of the heart, stress, or physical exhaustion, we must commit to fighting it. Anger can destroy our lives and our witness. We must recognize the unique ways in which anger affects us and wage war against it with all the seriousness and resolve that goes into fighting a battle. But we do not fight alone! We fight by engaging the almighty God in our battle and pray, asking for his help. The prayer of David in Psalm 141:3 is a good place to start: "Set a guard, O LORD, over my mouth; keep watch over the door of my lips!"

CHAPTER 15

LEARNING THE DISCIPLINE OF NOT RECKONING

1 CORINTHIANS 13:5D

I WILL NEVER FORGET a conversation I had with a member of the church where I had grown up. He had been hurt by another member many years earlier, and he made it clear to me that he would never be able to forgive this person for what he had done to him. "I will curse him on the day I die," he said to me. Though this is an extreme case of someone struggling with bitter resentment and unforgiveness, I hear milder forms of this resentment in conversations I have with people, expressed in statements like, "I have forgiven him, but I cannot forget what he did to me." The question we must consider is this: Are we able to move on after forgiving those who have wronged us, or do we keep a mental list of the ways people have hurt, offended, or wronged us?

Paul tells us, in 1 Corinthians 13:5d, that radical love does *not* keep a record of wrongs—it is not resentful or bitter, holding the past against those who have sinned against us. Instead, it focuses on the Lord's grace toward sinners, trusting that every wrong will be judged by God.

INTRODUCING A CHRISTIAN DISCIPLINE

There is an important Greek verb in this verse that has been translated in different ways. The ESV combines the verb with its object and reads: "Love ... is not ... resentful." This translation gives the sense of what Paul is saying. But I believe the NIV has the more literal sense because it focuses on the object of the verb ("wrongs"): "Love ... keeps no record of wrongs."

The Greek verb here is *logizomai*, which can be translated "consider, count, reckon or think." The most common use is "to keep a mental record of events for the sake of some future action."[1] It's an accounting word, referring to the logging of data or information in a book so that it can be recalled at any time. Paul is implying that we should *not* do this with the wrongs committed against us. Elsewhere, he uses this verb for the way God has shown his love for us in Christ: "in Christ God was reconciling the world to himself, not counting [*logizomai*] their trespasses against them" (2 Cor 5:19). Just as God forgives us and *treats us as if we have not sinned*, we should forgive people who have wronged us and treat them as if they have not done that.

To be clear, not reckoning a sin does not mean we try to forget details or pretend that the evil committed never happened. We are not supernaturally able to erase memories of wrongs done to us. But we can stop *reckoning* it—that is, we can stop looking at the wrong in a way that affects our present experience. We acknowledge that a wrong has been done, that it was bad and should not be excused. But as children of the God who is sovereign over everything that happens to us, we can see it as not having an adverse effect on us anymore. Just as those working on accounts throw away old files after five or six years, we decide to throw away the file that records this wrong done to us, affirming that it no longer has a significant bad affect on us.

But how does this work, especially when we have been deeply wounded or hurt? Again, I want to recall the two powerful truths we looked at in chapter 4. The first truth is that *God's love is greater than all the wrongdoing in the world*. Though the hurts that people inflict on us may be terrible, the love of God can heal those wounds through his comfort, provision, and loving concern for us that we will experience in different ways.

The second truth is that *God will turn even the hurtful things people have done to us into something good*. From a human perspective, such things hurt us, and we have a right to be angry and sad. But ultimately from God's perspective and from the perspective of sheer logic, there is no reason for us to think that this person has ruined us. God is greater than this person, and he will not allow somebody to irreparably hurt his child. Indeed, scars may remain; a mother whose husband left her for another woman may have to live as a single mother with all the sorrow of a failed marriage and all the challenge of bringing up a child without a father's presence. Yet, God can see her through and make something beautiful out of her life.

If God is going to turn the situation into something good, we must not block his work by reckoning evil — by continuing to meditate on the fact that this person has harmed us. Such meditation results in bitterness. It is bad fruit, borne of a lack of faith in the justice of God and the power of the Christ to overcome evil. We overcome sin, not by our own reckoning, but by affirming that God is bigger than this problem and he will heal and turn it to good. The temptation to bitterness hits all of us, for we are human. We struggle when we see those who commit evil prosper and succeed, and we question God's justice. So we must preach to ourselves that "for those who love God all things work together for good" (Rom. 8:28). We battle bitterness as an act of faith in the God whose love is greater than the unkindness of those who hurt us and whose power is greater than the harm done to us.

Nelson Mandela, who later became the great President of South Africa, was released in 1990 after serving twenty-seven years in prison. In the USA, his release was televised live, early in the morning. Bill Clinton, who later became President of his nation, woke up his daughter at three in the morning to witness this historic event. Years later, when he had the opportunity to speak to Mandela, he said to him, "As you marched from the cell block across the yard to the gate of the prison, the camera focused in on your face. I have never seen such anger, and even hatred, in any man as was expressed in your face at that time." Clinton then said, "That's not the Mandela I know today. What was all that about?"

After expressing regret that the cameras had caught his anger, Mandela said that as he walked across the courtyard that day, he was thinking to himself: "They've taken everything from you that matters. Your cause is dead. Your family is gone. Your friends have been killed. Now they're releasing you, but there's nothing left for you out there. And I hated them for what they had taken from me." But then, he says, he sensed an inner voice saying to him, "Nelson! For twenty-seven years you were their prisoner. But you were always a free man! Don't allow them to make you into a free man, only to turn you into their prisoner!" Mandela commented to Clinton: "An unforgiving spirit creates bitterness in our soul and imprisons our spirits. A failure to forgive imprisons us."[2]

It is impossible to forget the wrongs that have been done to us. Even if we have forgiven someone and are no longer reckoning the wrong done against us, we may find that when we see that person again, the first thing that comes to mind is what they did to us. In times like this, we must discipline ourselves to move past the memory and move forward in faith. Over time, after consistently choosing not to reckon the harm done to us, we may find that memory of it no longer comes to mind. Almost literally, we have forgotten the deed.

In chapter 6, I mentioned the British Methodist preacher William E. Sangster (1900–1960). Sangster preached and practiced a philosophy he described as "remembering to forget." Though he was often criticized, he tried to "remember to forget" the wrongs committed against him and focus on serving God instead. His wife once saw him addressing a Christmas card to someone and was shocked. She exclaimed, in disbelief, "Surely you are not sending a greeting to *him*!" She reminded him of something that man had done to him eighteen months earlier. In truth, Sangster had entirely forgotten the incident! He had actually remembered to forget![3]

Though it is possible for us to experience healing, there are still times when the memory of wounds we thought we were healed from will suddenly emerge to haunt us. This is also a natural thing for humans, and we should not grow discouraged or doubt the power of God to heal us. Life in this broken world will always be a battle of faith, and each time this happens we must learn to address our broken memories and emotions with our faith in God. Satan loves to have us meditate on pain from our past and will use every opportunity he can to dredge up old wounds and use them to ruin our lives. So we must act decisively to expel these thoughts from our minds when they threaten to recapture our thoughts. Martin Luther's words about dwelling on temptation are helpful here: "You cannot keep birds from flying over your head, but you can keep them from building a nest in your hair." We may suddenly remember hurtful things done to us, but we can refuse to entertain and nurture that memory.

In the previous chapter I mentioned that we would be looking at five triggers of anger in our lives, and we looked at the first three: carelessness, pressure and stress, and being physically weak. In the remainder of this chapter we will consider the final two: unresolved or hidden wounds from our past and a guilty conscience.

4. UNRESOLVED WOUNDS: PAIN FROM THE PAST

SEEKING RESOLUTION

There is a special challenge related to keeping no record of wrongs. This is the confusion that results from a conflict with another person or persons. It is important that we work on resolving anger and unresolved issues relating to conflicts we have had with others. Paul showed real wisdom when he said, "Be angry and do not sin; do not let the sun go down on your anger" (Eph. 4:26). If we keep our anger over unpleasant situations we've faced without dealing with it, it will surely emerge and express itself, often in the wrong place.

Many people leave jobs and churches angrily without talking about their anger to anyone in the organization or church they are leaving. They are on dangerous ground. When conflict comes up in their new church, what usually happens is that again they handle it inadequately and move to another church. I have seen people who have moved from church to church once they got into the habit of escaping the responsibility of facing up to their anger with others.

I believe in having exit interviews with staff workers who leave us. Sometimes those interviews are extremely painful to the leaders as those leaving say some nasty things. But they need to say them and get their anger out of their system. Otherwise they will carry it in their minds for a long time. They will keep scolding their former leaders in their minds but never get an opportunity to say it to them. The welfare of the people we lead is our responsibility, and that responsibility does not cease when staff workers are mad at us and are in the process of leaving. We have the responsibility to do everything we can to secure a good future for those who leave, regardless of their anger. The Bible does not give us the freedom to ignore the needs of such brothers and sisters!

Sometimes we cannot talk directly to the people who have hurt us. They may be unwilling to talk or be inaccessible. In such cases we should talk to someone else and work to clear it out in our minds. Someone once hurt me deeply by making serious accusations against me. An inquiry exonerated me, but for several months I could not get away from the anger I had with this person. I shared this with my friends, and they suggested that, in keeping with biblical teaching, I try to meet the person. I did try, but he was not willing to meet me. The moment I made that effort, the burden left me. I had done what I could and placed the heavy load of anger on the Lord. He freed me. Paul wrote, "If possible, so far as it depends on you, live peaceably with all" (Rom. 12:18). He recognized that we cannot make peace with some people. The honest effort to resolve the issue automatically frees us from its burden and allows grace to heal the wound.

We must be careful when working with people with unresolved conflicts. Their anger can come out in a tense situation, and they can act in ways that are destructive. In a delightful book of letters by C. John Miller, we find this warning: "Do be very careful about giving power positions or roles of influence to leaders who leave behind them a record of unreconciled conflicts. Believe me, in one hasty day you can undo years of your own hard work."[4]

I can summarize one of the most important teachings of this chapter with these words: *Don't go through life with unresolved wounds!*

HURTS BURIED IN THE SUBCONSCIOUS

There are some situations where the suggestions and advice I have just shared do not seem to work. Sometimes the wounds are buried so deep in the subconscious that, despite love for God that a person has, they continue to exhibit reactions that show that there is further need for healing. Early in my ministry I read a book by Dr. David Seamands, *Healing for Damaged Emotions*, in which he said, "Whenever you experience a response on your part that is way out of proportion to the stimulus, then look out. You have probably tapped into some deeply hidden emotional hurt." Seamands tells the story of a professor in a Bible college who was a learned biblical scholar. A confrontation with another person at the college led this professor to react in violent anger, so much so that the professor himself was shocked at his response. He admitted to Dr. Seamands : "I actually felt as if I wanted to go out and kill somebody."

As Seamands talked with this professor, he learned that as a child "he was always first in the classroom but last on the playground." Because of his ineptness in sports, he was brutally bullied by his classmates, both boys and girls. As he was relating the story, the man "was amazed at the sensitivity of his memory." He could remember each of the children by name, even down to the details of what they were wearing. He found that there was a huge, hidden rage that had lain dormant within him for many years. The hidden rage in his heart had been uncovered through the confrontation at the college, and Dr. Seamands was able to lead this man through a process of forgiving each of the people who had hurt him. This helped open the door for the Holy Spirit to apply his healing balm to his wounds, and over time this brought peace to the underlying rage in his life.[5]

On occasion in my ministry I have encountered situations where I sensed that there were damaged emotions in need of healing. As I described in chapter 5, after identifying the specific wounds a person is struggling with, we usually prepare a service of healing for this person and possibly his or her spouse. If the hurt person is a woman, I bring my wife along to assist. I have the person write down a description of each wound in some detail and come for the service with that written document in hand. After a time of prayer, the person reads each description and I respond to what they have written with a response grounded in the Scriptures that addresses that wound. Then, the person spends some time praying a prayer forgiving the person who has hurt him or her. Sadly, in most of these situations, it is the person's parents who need to be forgiven. After praying through each wound and forgiving the person who wronged them, we burn the paper in which the hurts are recorded as a sign that they are leaving this memory permanently in the past. I have seen God using this process to bring healing to hurt people.

People need help surfacing their wounds so that the healing grace of God can be applied to them. If you find you are in need of this right now, as you read, I would urge you to find someone who can help you, such a pastor, a close friend you trust, or a counselor, to walk you through a process of healing.

5. A GUILTY CONSCIENCE: FAILING TO GRASP THE GOSPEL OF GRACE

The fifth and final reason why people are prone to anger is a guilty conscience. It is only marginally related to the text we are studying in this chapter: not keeping a record of wrong. However, I insert it here as a special note as the earlier chapter (where it should have been) got too long! People who struggle with a guilty conscience lose the peace of God. Earlier, we saw that Paul spoke of this peace *guarding* our hearts and our minds in Christ Jesus (Phil. 4:7) and *ruling* in our hearts (Col. 3:15). In other words, because peace is one of the qualities that characterizes the life of a Christian, the loss of peace is a sure sign that there is a problem in our relationship with God. David sensed this loss of fellowship after he fell into serious sin. He prayed, "Restore to me the joy of your salvation" (Ps. 51:12). Sin breaks our fellowship with God, which in turn results in the loss of our peace and joy. When joy and peace are lacking, we easily grow irritable.

David Seamands talks about a young minister who was having problems getting along with others, especially with his wife and family. He was always criticizing his wife, and even his sermons were harsh and judgmental. As Seamands comments, "He was working out all of his unhappiness on other people." After meeting for awhile with Seamands, the painful root of his problem came to light. When he was engaged to be married, he had been stationed in Korea while serving in the US armed forces. He had two weeks of holiday (R and R) time, which he chose to spend in Tokyo, Japan. During that leave, while walking the streets of Tokyo and feeling empty, lonely, and terribly homesick, he fell into temptation and went three or four times to a prostitute.

He could not forgive himself for what he had done, and he did not have the assurance that God had forgiven him. He eventually returned home to marry his fiancée, never telling her what had happened, but because of his hidden sin he had a difficult time accepting her love for him. He was living in what A. W. Tozer once called "the perpetual penance of regret." Thankfully, the story has a beautiful ending. He was able to accept God's forgiveness and receive forgiveness from his wife as well as from himself.[6] He had to come to a place where he was no longer "reckoning his sin" against himself, choosing instead to believe the good news that he was now forgiven and accepted by God.

In Psalm 32:1 David writes, "Blessed is the one whose transgression is forgiven, whose sin is covered." Yet before grasping the joy and happiness that come from knowing the good news of God's grace and forgiveness, David had a time of inner turmoil: "For when I kept silent, my bones wasted away through my groaning all day long" (32:3). Keeping his sin hidden caused him great turmoil and pain—even physical pain—until he finally came to accept and confess his sin: "I acknowledged my sin to you, and I did not cover my iniquity; I said, 'I will confess my transgressions to the LORD.'" The result was freedom: "and you forgave the iniquity of my sin" (32:5).

How important it is for us to keep "short accounts" with God. When you know you have failed, the *only* path to healing is to go to God in sorrowful confession. John reminds us of this when he tells us that if "we confess our sins, he is faithful and just to forgive us our sins and to cleanse us from all unrighteousness" (1 John 1:9). No sin is greater than the grace God extends to us through the work of Christ. God is "faithful" in keeping his promise to forgive our sin, and he is "just" in doing so because Jesus paid the penalty for it! So don't let the account pertaining to our sin drag on for long; go to him at once and receive the freedom of his forgiveness.

, , ,

We have looked at two final ways in which we can keep the truth of the gospel in our hearts and avoid the trap of anger. Radical love keeps no record of wrong, and so we must be careful to release the wrongs committed against us, trusting God to turn this painful situation into something good. Yet we must also recognize that we are susceptible to the power of guilt and shame in our own lives. Sometimes, we must learn to "forgive ourselves" by returning to the good news of the gospel and allowing the powerful truth of our undeserved and unearned acceptance before God to penetrate deep into our hearts. We must confess our sin and allow God's faithful and just forgiveness to release us from guilt.

Sin will destroy your peace and make you prone to anger. Jesus has the power to set you free. That is that very reason he came to this world and died and rose again: "It is for freedom that Christ has set us free. Stand firm, then, and do not let yourselves be burdened again by a yoke of slavery" (Gal. 5:1 NIV). The radical love of God empowers us to stand firm against the power of sin, freely offering forgiveness to others and accepting God's forgiveness of our own sin.

CHAPTER 16

LOVE FOCUSES ON THE TRUTH, NOT ON WRONG

1 CORINTHIANS 13:6

WHAT GIVES YOU the greatest thrill? What makes you happy and leads you to rejoice? In 1 Corinthians 13:6, Paul tells us that those who are filled with God's love will find their joy, not in sin, but in the truth: "[Love] does not rejoice at wrongdoing, but rejoices with the truth." When God's love is the foundation for our thoughts and our emotions and the guiding motive behind our decisions, we will naturally find ourselves thrilled when good things happen to people and the truth of God is revealed in their lives.

We will likewise be upset at evil and sin and at the hypocrisy and selfishness we see in ourselves and in others. Because we live in a broken world and relate to others in our brokenness, it's inevitable that we will be hurt and disappointed by sin and evil. Many people, even Christians, can grow cynical about the idea of goodness. They have a difficult time rejoicing in the good they see because they are afraid that it isn't real, or they fear it won't last. In a world of counterfeits and broken promises, they find it hard to believe there is anything worth celebrating.

The love of God in our hearts battles such cynicism. It seeks the best for everyone and is genuinely happy when something good happens and genuinely sad when something bad happens. We will be disappointed by the behavior of some people, but we refuse to give up on the idea that goodness is possible. At times, we may be confronted by pain so great that we are tempted to adopt a clinical approach to deal with it. We may attempt to keep our pain at a distance, trying hard not to allow the evil of this world to influence our emotions. We may try to insulate ourselves by avoiding situations and circumstances where we would risk being hurt. When God's love fills our lives, we have strength to take the risk of being happy about good things in the lives of others. Even if they prove to be a disappointment in the end, the love of God in us braces us with strength to take on that disappointment.

God's love in us also gives us the strength to take on the pain of being broken by bad things in the lives of others. We know that though we make ourselves vulnerable in this way and allow ourselves to be broken, the most important and beautiful things in our lives are not dislodged. These are the beautiful love of God and the joy that comes from experiencing this love.

CHRISTIANITY CAN INCREASE OUR PAIN

Sometimes, our suffering can actually increase after we become a Christian. Consider a person who has left home and avoids his father because of deep resentment and pain from his childhood. He learns to cope with his pain and live a relatively successful life by insulating his mind and emotions from the truth about his relationship with his father. Yet after he becomes a Christian, he now realizes he needs to reach out and try relating to his father, even showing love to him. This experience is difficult for him, as it opens up a plethora of painful and buried emotions. It is a process that must be handled gently; we must make sure the person is mature and strong enough to handle it. He needs constant, specific reminders that God's love will give him the strength he needs to bear the pain, as well as encouragement and hope in the power of the gospel to change and transform broken relationships and save broken people.

I will never forget a call that I received from the wife of a good friend one Sunday night. She informed me, sadly, that she had received reliable news that a couple my wife and I had ministered to (at some personal cost) had deceived us and had done some terrible things that we had not been told about.

That night, I found it difficult to fall sleep. After lying awake for an hour or two, I went to the room that serves as my home office, thinking that I might as well do some study. A fax had come in from the organizers of the Urbana Student Missions Conference in the US, where I was scheduled to give several Bible expositions. The fax mentioned four passages they wanted me to talk about, and one of them was John 10, so I decided to study it.

I pulled out one of my favorite books on the gospel of John, *Reflections on the Gospel of John* by Leon Morris, and read his comments on John 10:11–21. Morris pointed out that when Jesus calls himself "the good shepherd," he uses a Greek word for "good" that "refers to what is *beautiful* as well as what is good" (emphasis mine). Morris went on to quote a translation by the classical scholar E. V. Rieu, which translates John 10:11 this way: "I am the shepherd, the shepherd beautiful."[1]

My mind began to race as I thought about the beauty of Jesus as the shepherd of his flock. I had been struggling to sleep because I was feeling betrayed. I kept telling myself that I would never trust people again, as I had done with this couple. But now, after reading this passage in John, I was thinking to myself: "How can I be cynical when my heart has been softened by the amazing love of the good shepherd? He has beautifully demonstrated his love for me by dying on the cross." I realized that the love that God had showered on me was far greater than the betrayal I felt.

I also remembered David's words in Psalm 27:4, words written as he faced hostility from his enemies and painful rejection from his own family: "One thing have I asked of the LORD, that will I seek after: that I may dwell in the house of the LORD all the days of my life, to gaze upon the beauty of the LORD and to inquire in his temple." As we gaze on the beauty of our crucified Lord, it dispels our cynicism and replaces it with sorrow over evil and joy over truth!

Yes, it is painful to be betrayed. It is difficult to be deceived, and there is terrible evil in this world. But God's love is greater than the evil we experience. He overcame evil on the cross, and after receiving his grace that flows from Calvary, we need to look at all people through the eyes of the cross. People can be transformed through the grace that flows from the cross. When we see evil we mourn, but we mourn with a longing to see those responsible transformed by the righteousness of God. And when we see goodness, we genuinely rejoice—not because we believe in the inherent goodness of people, but because we believe in the power of God to use imperfect people to accomplish real, genuine good. It all comes down to a matter of focus, of what we choose to believe. Will we look at the evil and goodness we see in this world through the lens of the gospel?

REFUSING TO REJOICE AT WRONGDOING

In the first part of 1 Corinthians 13:6, Paul says, "[Love] does not rejoice at wrongdoing." What David Hocking says about this is sadly true: "It's easy to be glad at another person's misfortune when it makes you look better."[2] Finding happiness in the problems of others is clear evidence of our own feelings of inadequacy and insecurity. We try to compensate for our own weakness by focusing on the weaknesses of others. Their failures give us some satisfaction because we use that to buttress the idea that we are not as bad as they are. Looking at them, we feel better about ourselves.

We've all probably met people who inspire us to say something bad about someone else. It is an almost automatic reaction when we meet this person; we are prompted to tell him something bad about someone. Why? Because we know that these people thrive on bad news. They may even be proud of this, claiming to be "watchdogs" against immorality and hypocrisy.

One of the saddest examples of rejoicing at wrongdoing is when a Christian finds inner satisfaction from the failings of other Christians. I refer to this as an *inner* satisfaction because we may speak to others about these failures under the cloak of prayer or concern, while inwardly we find satisfaction from talking about those failings. When the pastor of a nearby church falls into sin, we should weep inside, not gloat over his failure! We need to remember that this is a part of our own body. When the thumb is hurt by a hammer that lands on it rather than on the nail it was aiming at (sadly, a common occurrence in my life), it is the foot that jumps and the throat that screams in pain. "If one part suffers, every part suffers with it; if one part is honored, every part rejoices with it" (1 Cor. 12:26).

Since our identity comes from belonging to Christ, we don't need to base our self-image on how bad other people are in comparison to us. Instead, we must grab hold of our identity and significance as children of God who have been gifted to do significant things that are of eternal value. In chapter 9 we looked at how envy is caused by a lack of identity and significance, and we examined about how we can restore this understanding in our lives. If we are happy and secure in our relationship with God, we no longer need to seek our self-worth by comparing ourselves to others.

One of the most common ways in which we rejoice in the wrongdoing and suffering of others is through gossip. There is an almost universal desire among people to be entertained by hearing how others have failed. Gossip can become an addiction, something we have trouble controlling. People with an addiction to gossip often do not take into account the consequences of their behavior. Sometimes Christians gossip about the failures of Christians leaders in company that would be harmed by such disclosures. They expose the scandals and conflicts in the church by openly sharing them with people who are not Christians. Without a proper context for understanding the details, such conversations can turn people away from considering the gospel. Sometimes scandal mongers peddle their gossip before new believers, who are not yet ready to bear the burden of knowing that terrible things can happen in the church. Gossip is speech that is not motivated by love but by a selfishness that exploits the sins of others.

Instead of being entertained or comforted by the sins of others, we should mourn. Love wants to see others doing the best they can by the grace of God, whereas gossip does the opposite, revealing their flaws. First Peter 4:8 says that love has the power to cover sin — not to hide it but to nullify its power and limit its effects: "Above all, keep loving one another earnestly, since love covers a multitude of sins." To cover sin is to refuse to use it in public. As we have seen, there are times when we need to discipline those who have sinned and share about their sin with others in the community of faith. But there is a key difference between this type of sharing and gossip. Sharing for the intent of discipline is done out of love for the person and for the health of the group to which he or she belongs.

Those of us who counsel others often know things about people that would make for juicy gossip. We intentionally do not share these details. I am typically quite free in sharing details of my day and my ministry with my wife. But we have a rule that I will not share with her anything embarrassing that I learn about someone through counseling or sharing. I am especially strict about not sharing anything relating to the sexual behavior of a man. Sometimes, we find ourselves in a situation where people are discussing an individual and what he has done, and it is clear that they do not know all of the facts in the case. We may know more details because we have counseled the person. In circumstances like this, we will pretend not to know because we must keep such things confidential.

When it comes to our enemies, the Bible tells us that we are to love them (Matt. 5:44; Luke 6:27, 35; Rom. 12:20). That means we should not gloat over their defeats or over humiliating exposures of their sins. A young man named Jonathan was a lay leader in one of our Asian churches. He was guilty of a "minor" indiscretion for which he was disciplined by the church. Then, the news came out that the person who had acted as "prosecutor" in his discipline was guilty of a far more serious sin. When Jonathan's uncle heard the news, he openly expressed great delight over this man's failure. Many of us would likely respond in the same way, wouldn't we? Yet why do we find such delight in the failures and sins of others?

It is natural for us initially to wish that a person who hurt us "will learn a lesson," which really means that we wish for the person to suffer in some way. But gradually love does its work to change those vengeful desires to a wish that he would repent. Of course, it is right for us also to desire that the effects on us of his evil action would be taken away. For example, if we have been falsely slandered, it is right for us to act in order to clear our name.

REJOICING WITH THE TRUTH

The second part of 1 Corinthians 13:6 gives us the other side of the coin. Not only does love *not* rejoice in sin and evil, but it actively "rejoices with the truth." The truth Paul is referring to is a contrast to unsubstantiated gossip. We are people who live under the lordship of a God who speaks truth. His truth delights and thrills us. As the psalmists declare, we delight in the Word of God (Pss. 1:2; 19:7–10; 119:14, 16, 24, 35, etc.). When we encounter things relating to what we delight in, we will rejoice. That is a natural response. Again, can you see how the feature of love that we are studying is the result of focusing on the right things?

In his letter to the Philippians Paul vividly clarifies the kinds of things a Christian should focus on: "Finally, brothers, whatever is true, whatever is honorable, whatever is just, whatever is pure, whatever is lovely, whatever is commendable, if there is any excellence, if there is anything worthy of praise, think about these things. What you have learned and received and heard and seen in me—practice these things, and the God of peace will be with you" (Phil. 4:8–9). Notice too that just prior to giving us this list of things to think about, Paul describes how the peace of God will guard us (4:7). Then, at the end of this list he talks of "the God of peace" being with us (4:9). When our anger with life is healed, we have the peace of God. Then we can focus on things that are compatible with that peace. We become people who love the progress of truth and rejoice when they see this progress.

One of the greatest joys in life is hearing news that someone we know has been saved by the truth of the gospel and has come home to the family of God. Luke records three lost-and-found parables in Luke 15. After relating each of the first two parables, Jesus gives us a window into the activities of heaven, that when a sinner repents there is great rejoicing in heaven (15:7, 10). The third story likewise speaks of a huge celebration with music and dancing and a feast after the lost son returns home (15:23–25). The best thing that can happen to anyone is for that person to accept the truth, meet the Savior of the world, and experience his salvation. When this happens, it should thrill our hearts. If we ever cease to be thrilled when people come to God and receive salvation, this is a sure sign that we are in desperate need of revival. We are thrilled in this way because we are thrilled with what the gospel is and does!

William Tyndale (1494–1536), an English reformer, was convinced that English-speaking people needed to have the Bible in their own language. Thus, he translated the New Testament and portions of the Old Testament into English. For doing this, he was arrested in Brussels and put to death as a martyr by being strangled and having his body burned at the stake. In the preface to his English translation of the New Testament, Tyndale described the word "gospel," which "signified good, merry, glad and joyful tidings, that make a person's heart glad, and make him sing, dance and leap for joy."[3] Tyndale understood the joy of the truth of the gospel!

We live in what has been called the postmodern age, a time when people seem to have lost their trust in objective truth. People see things like doctrine and absolute truth as outdated and irrelevant, beliefs that enslave people and restrict their freedom. Many people today place greater value on the latest technology over doctrinal truth. Talking about the *joy* of truth may sound strange to the ears of many people. People don't usually place much value on things like meditating on the truth or having holy conversations about the things of God. They rush through life, working hard to make a living; and when they want a break from that, they turn to the entertainment industry to provide them with stress-reducing diversions.

Christians live differently. We believe that real fulfillment in life comes through understanding the truth. This is a truth that has been revealed by the Creator of the world, a truth we can read in God's written Word, a truth that is most clearly seen in the person of Jesus. Jesus himself said, "You will know the truth, and the truth will set you free" (John 8:32). This truth is delightful, for it opens the way to a feast of pleasure prepared for us by God.

Francis of Assisi (1182–1226) once said, "To him who tastes God, all the sweetness of the world will be but bitterness."[4] When we have tasted of Christ and the joy of his truth, we will want to talk about it, think about it, read about it, and study it. However, the mood of the day can influence us in the opposite direction: to undervalue truth. Paul warns us of this by commanding us: "Do not conform to the pattern of this world, but be transformed by the renewing of your mind" (Rom. 12:2 NIV). We resist the influence of the world by *renewing* our minds. One way to do that is to stop from our busy activity to enjoy truth.

This past year I preached in a church near Oxford, England, and had the memorable experience of touring the city. I am immensely proud of a photo that my host, the Rev. Gareth Lloyd Jones, took of me beside a pub in Oxford called "The Eagle and Child." Meeting in this pub, the great Christian novelist and writer C. S. Lewis (author of *The Chronicles of Narnia*) and his friends, including the famous literary figures J. R. R. Tolkien (author of *The Lord of the Rings* and *The Hobbit*) and Charles Williams, would gather every week to talk and converse with one another. Lewis found great joy in these times; in writing about his delight in their conversations, he says:

> He is lucky beyond desert to be in such company. Especially when the whole group is together, each bringing out all that is best, wisest, or funniest in all the others. Those are the golden sessions; when four of us after a hard day's walking have come to our inn; when our slippers are on, our feet spread out toward the blaze and our drinks at our elbows; when the whole world, and something beyond the world, opens itself to our minds as we talk; and no one has any claim on or any responsibility for another, but all are freemen and equals as if we had first met an hour ago, while at the same time an affection mellowed by the years enfolds us. Life — natural life — has no better gift to give. Who could have deserved it?[5]

I have an accountability group of five friends (down from six after one died) who have known each other for almost forty-five years. At one time or another, each of us has been involved in the ministry of Youth for Christ, though now I am the only Youth for Christ staff worker in the group. We meet once a month, typically for three to four hours. Some of our time is spent sharing how we are faring in our spiritual walk with the Lord. We talk about how we have fared in our areas of weakness and struggle against sin. But most of our time is spent just chatting. We talk about a wide variety of topics, including theology, politics, sports, the books we have been reading, and what we have been learning from our Bible reading. All this is done from a Christian perspective. Sometimes we stray into the area of gossip, and we have to ask God to forgive us. This group has been a source of life and joy to me over the years, regularly refreshing my soul.

Some of the happiest memories in my ministry came while making a weekly trip of about an hour and a half to our drug rehab center. Usually, one of our staff accompanied me on the trip. Most of the journey was spent talking together: talking about the Lord, talking about our experiences and challenges, talking about the lessons we have learned recently — and a host of other topics.

Do you have opportunities to engage in "holy" conversation with other believers? May your small groups be loaded with discussions on biblical texts and on issues facing Christians from a biblical perspective! Talk to your friends about what you have discovered through reading the Word recently. This is also a wonderful way for husbands and wives to enjoy each other and affirm that their union is based on God's Word, not the changing circumstances of life. If couples talk only about the challenges faced by the family, they should not be surprised if their home is a gloomy place. While we do talk about our challenges, the focus of conversation between Christian husbands and wives should be on the beautiful truths relating to our God and his Word.

, , ,

We can choose the focus of our conversation and thinking. Whatever our vocation, our hobbies, or the topics that capture our interest may be, may the underlying focus in our thinking and talking be on God, his love, his holiness, and his truth. May all our thinking be sent through that grid. Then almost subconsciously we will become people who do not rejoice at wrongdoing, but rejoice with the truth.

We kick the habit of gossip and gloating over the wrongs we see in others by discovering the joy of truth, by lingering with truth, and by engaging in holy conversation that is based on truth. In other words, there is deep and abiding fulfillment in handling eternal truth.

CHAPTER 17

LOVE'S PERSEVERANCE

1 CORINTHIANS 13:7

WE LIVE IN A WORLD where we have the ability to find instant solutions to many of our problems. When I was studying in the United States in the mid–70s, the cost of making a phone call home to Sri Lanka was simply too high to justify making calls. Even when my mother underwent major surgery, it was too expensive for me, living on a student budget. To get any news from home, I had to call my brother who lived in the US at the time. Because he was employed, he could afford to call home and would relay the news to me. Those student years were an emotionally difficult time for me, but with God's help I was able to cope.

Today, things are so different! Making an international call is as easy as talking to someone in the next room at home. But with these wonderful advances in technology and travel, I have also noticed that it is easier for people to circumvent experiences that would have once shaped their spiritual growth and development.

Consider a student from an affluent country who decides to commit to a six-month missionary assignment in an economically less-developed nation. She has good intentions, but soon discovers that her living conditions are quite basic—not at all what she was prepared for. She struggles to cope, lacking the comforts of home. She calls home every day and tells her parents about her struggles. Her parents get upset and blame the organization for sending her to "this terrible place." They demand that she return home immediately. Though her return home alleviates her short-term discomfort, in reality she has now missed out on a wonderful opportunity to learn, mature in her faith, and take further steps of spiritual growth.

The ability to find near instantaneous relief for pain and discomfort and an epidemic of addiction to immediate gratification make it difficult for people to develop the two qualities of love we will discuss in this chapter: perseverance and endurance.

TWO SIMILAR VERBS

First Corinthians 13:7 adopts a literary form that scholars refer to as a *chiasmus*. In a chiasmus, pairs of similar statements are arranged in a reversed structure, what can be described as an "A-B-B-A" sequence.

A Love bears all things,
  B believes all things,
  B' hopes all things,
A' endures all things.

In this example, "bears" is parallel with "endures," and "believes" is parallel with "hopes." So as we unpack the meaning of this verse, we will be considering these parallel characteristics of love together. For the remainder of this chapter, we'll look at the *persevering* nature of love—that it "bears" and "endures." In the next chapter, we'll consider the *hopeful* nature of love—that it "believes" and "hopes."

In considering the persevering nature of love, we should first note that the first word Paul uses can be translated as "bears" (ESV) or "protects" (NIV). If the meaning is "protects," it communicates the idea of keeping something confidential or passing over it in silence (not drawing attention to it). It would have a meaning similar to what we find in 1 Peter 4:8b, where Peter tells us that "love covers a multitude of sins." However, in our verse, it is more likely that the idea of love "bearing" all things is closer to the nuance of enduring or persevering. In the other three occurrences of this verb (*stegō*) in the New Testament, all of which are in Paul's letters (1 Cor. 9:12; 1 Thess. 3:1, 5), the nuance is closer to that of "enduring." This matches the chiasmus as well and seems the most likely intention of Paul in this section.

While *stegō* appears only four times in the New Testament, the other verb in the couplet, "endures" (*hypomenō*), is a far more common word, appearing seventeen times. Barclay translates the sense of this verse by saying that love "bears everything with triumphant fortitude."[1] The notion of love enduring communicates a sense of triumphant perseverance amidst trials. It can be used in the context of a battlefield to refer to "the attitude of the soldier who in the thick of the battle is not dismayed but fights on stoutly whatever the difficulties."[2] Barclay tells the story of the great Scottish preacher and hymn writer George Matheson. Matheson went blind in his youth and was disappointed in love. In one of his written prayers, he asked for grace that he might accept God's will: "not with dumb resignation but with holy joy; not only with the absence of murmur but with a song of praise."[3] That's the sense of enduring, persevering love that Paul is trying to communicate here; it takes a positive approach to problems stemming from a firm confidence in God's sovereignty over the circumstances of life.

PERSEVERANCE AND HOPE

How is it possible for us to have this kind of positive attitude of endurance or perseverance when the world around us seems to be falling to pieces? Paul says this is possible because we have hope. Endurance is connected with hope in Romans 8:25. In the previous verses Paul talked about the frustration that followers of Christ encounter along with the rest of creation and how that triggers groaning as we await our final redemption (8:18–23). Later he says that "we know that for those who love God all things work together for good" (8:28). So we await the final redemption and we know that all things will work together for good. What do we do in the meantime? Verse 25 says we persevere or endure with hope: "But if we hope for what we do not see, we wait for it with patience." Paul uses the noun (*hypomenē*) here, which is parallel to the verb (*hypomenō*) that Paul uses in the verse we are studying. Paul teaches that amidst hardships, we don't give up; we continue with patience, knowing (in hope) that something good will come out of it.

The good that Romans 8:28 talks about is that as a result of the experience, we will "be conformed to the image of his Son, in order that he might be the firstborn among many brothers" (8:29). We become like Jesus, and when that happens, our true identity as the brothers of Jesus shines through. While Jesus was always our brother, now because we have become like him, we are truly what God made us to be. We become fulfilled, contented people. Elsewhere Paul said that "godliness with contentment is great gain" (1 Tim. 6:6). Henry Clay Morrison, the founder of Asbury

Theological Seminary, where I studied, used to say, "God never fixed me up so that I couldn't sin. He fixed me up so that I couldn't sin and enjoy it." Our frustrating experiences make us more like Christ, which in turn makes us contented people.

James describes the purifying process of difficulties: "Count it all joy, my brothers, when you meet trials of various kinds, for you know that the testing of your faith produces steadfastness. And let steadfastness have its full effect, that you may be perfect and complete, lacking in nothing" (Jas. 1:2–4; see also Rom. 5:3–4). The noun translated "steadfastness" is *hypomenē* (see above). So as we go through trials, we can persevere knowing that God is doing something good in our lives through them. We do not give up the battle but we persevere, putting our hope in God not only to see us through but also to do something good out of this situation.

WE WILL NOT GIVE IN OR GIVE UP

Though the descriptions of love "bearing" all things and "enduring" all things are closely related, connected by the idea of perseverance, there seem to be subtle differences between the two words. In a recent commentary on 1 Corinthians, Roy Ciampa and Brian Rosner suggest that the first word ("bears") could connote the idea that a person "won't give *in*." The second word ("endures") may suggest that a person "won't give *up*" (emphasis added).[4]

What is the difference between giving *in* and giving *up*? Love gives *in* when it fails to hold fast to the truth and caves into the pressures of the world. Sometimes it can seem foolish, particularly in our culture of instant gratification, to choose the costly path of self-denial and commitment to God and people. Sometimes even people close to us think we are fools when we follow a costly path. Someone who works with drug addicts and sees failure after failure is challenged by his parents to "give up this folly and do something useful" with his life. A Christian is being slandered by someone she has counseled; she knows a lot of sordid stories of sin in this other person's life, but she refuses to divulge those stories. Yet the other person continues to slander her name. How much pressure there is for her to drop some hints about this person's previous life of sin. Christian love refuses to give in to wrong ways to solve a problem.

Love also refuses to give *up* when the going gets tough. People often give up on others, abandoning their commitments and promises because they can no longer handle them. Over the years, there have been many times when I have struggled with discouragement. Sometimes, it was because of the reaction of a staff person, disagreeing with my leadership and the direction I felt God was leading us to go. Sometimes I felt like giving up and moving on to another ministry.

I remember one day when I was struggling with all of this as I was preparing to preach on the call of Isaiah. In my message, I was going to share how God's call to Isaiah included a rather strange promise: the very people he was sent to minister to would reject him and his message (Isa. 6:9–10). Isaiah, knowing what lay ahead, went on to serve the people, even though they opposed him and finally killed him (tradition tells us that he was sawn in two).

Yet how glad we are today that Isaiah persevered! We have the priceless treasure of the book of Isaiah. What struck me that day, when I was so discouraged, was that it was not the people who called Isaiah to his ministry—it was God. That is why he could not give up and quit, even though people had rejected him. Isaiah understood that he could not leave his ministry until God released him. Rejection was irrelevant; God's calling was clear. I realized that day that whatever the people do to me, if God called me to Youth for Christ, then I must not give up until God calls me to leave. After thirty-six years I have still not heard that call to leave!

Dwight L. Moody (1837–1899) was possibly the most prominent evangelist in the world during his time, and he began his ministry in Chicago working among the poor. Moody struggled with discouragement from time to time when he could not see any noticeable fruit in his ministry. A Sunday school teacher once saw that he was discouraged, and when Moody shared his struggle, the teacher asked him if he had ever read the story of Noah. Moody mentioned that he was quite familiar with the story, yet the man persisted: "If you never studied that carefully, you ought to do it; for I cannot tell you what a blessing it has been to me."

Curious, Moody began to read the story, and as he did so, he felt a weight lifting. "Here is a man that toiled and worked a hundred years and didn't get discouraged," he thought to himself. For Moody, it was as if the clouds suddenly lifted: "I got up and said, 'If the Lord wants me to work without any fruit, I will work on.'"

He then went to a noon prayer meeting, and as he saw a crowd of people coming to pray, he was reminded of Noah: "Noah worked for a hundred years, and he never saw a prayer meeting outside his own family." A man at that meeting shared a testimony that a hundred people had joined the church in the past year. Moody told himself, "What if Noah had heard that! He preached so many, many years and didn't get a single convert; yet he was not discouraged." Another man got up and asked for Moody to pray for his soul. Moody said, "What if Noah had heard that! He worked 120 years and he never had a man come to him and say that; yet he did not get discouraged."

Moody realized that he was far too concerned about things that were under God's control, and he committed to fighting his discouragement with faith in God. "I made up my mind then that, God helping me, I would never get discouraged. I would do the best I could and leave the results with God; and it has been a wonderful help to me."[5]

We all struggle with discouragement. It's normal to be tempted to quit and give up when we face a difficult task. In the record in Joshua 1 of Joshua's call to lead in place of Moses, God tells Joshua *four times* that he needs to be strong and not grow discouraged (Josh. 1:6, 7, 9, 18). We also see that this same command was given twice to Joshua in Deuteronomy 31 — by Moses (Deut 31:7) and by God (31:23). Clearly, fighting against discouragement is an important aspect of leadership! Most importantly, we should notice that in all six instances where Joshua is commanded to be strong, his strength is directly related to the presence and help of God.

, , ,

How do we develop a persevering quality to our love? As we saw earlier, James gives us a clue to this when he talks about the trials we face, that "the testing of your faith produces steadfastness" (Jas. 1:3). As we said earlier in this chapter, "steadfastness" is the noun form of the verb translated as "endures" in 1 Corinthians 13:7. In his letter to the Romans, Paul uses this noun form when he says that "suffering produces endurance" (Rom. 5:3). In both of these passages, we see that endurance (or perseverance) is something that is learned and developed *through suffering or trials*. Both James 1:2–3 and Romans 5:3 tell us that we should be happy about the trials because through them we develop endurance.

The ability to endure hardship with a confident attitude, trusting in God, is one of the greatest gifts a person can have. The happiest people in the world are not those who have no problems. They are those who are not afraid of problems. So trials take on a decidedly positive tenor with this understanding that trials are the means through which we receive one of the most important qualities in a happy life — endurance.

A man came to his pastor and asked for prayer that he would be more patient at home. The pastor began to pray and kept saying, "Send my brother tribulation." After a little of this the man patted the pastor on the back and said, "But, Pastor, I did not ask for tribulation, I asked for patience." The pastor replied, "Ah, but 'tribulation worketh patience'" (see KJV of Rom. 5:3).

CHAPTER 18

GRACE-FILLED: NEITHER GULLIBLE NOR CYNICAL

1 CORINTHIANS 13:7

A FEW DAYS BEFORE writing this chapter, I was asked to preach at the funeral of a good friend, Raja Wijekoon. Raja pioneered the ministry of Christian drug rehabilitation in Sri Lanka, and I got to know him well as I serve as an advisor to the consortium of Christian drug rehab agencies in Sri Lanka. Raja was converted in prison while serving a sentence for armed robbery. He was given a Bible, and as he was reading he was struck by the words, "Come to me, all who labor and are heavy laden, and I will give you rest" (Matt. 11:28). This invitation led him to yield his life to Christ. After his release from prison, he began a ministry with drug dependents.

Before I spoke, there were testimonies from three former drug dependents who had all been delivered from their addiction through Raja's ministry and were now leading responsible Christian lives. They all spoke of how Raja had graciously accepted them back, even after they had returned to drugs. One man shared that he had ten relapses into his addiction before finally experiencing lasting freedom. Every time he returned to the rehab center, Raja took him back in the hope that this would be the last time.

In the last chapter we looked at the first and fourth (or last) statements of what we called a chiasmus in 1 Corinthians 13:7 — how Christian love "bears all things" and "endures all things." We talked about the need for perseverance, and how God uses trials and suffering in our lives to develop our ability to love others with a love that endures — neither giving *in* when faced with the temptation to compromise nor giving *up* when faced with setbacks and disappointments. Now we will consider the middle two qualities Paul uses to describe love in this verse: "Love ... believes all things, hopes all things" (13:7). As we will see, Paul is talking here about a settled disposition of goodwill toward people. The NIV captures this sense by translating the passage, "Love ... always trusts, always hopes." In other words, Christian love is radical because it gives people the benefit of the doubt. It is willing to take people at their word, seeing the best in them despite the reality of sin in their lives. Christians are *grace-filled* people.

A GRACE-FILLED ATTITUDE TO PEOPLE

When Paul presents belief and hope as descriptions of love, he is presumably referring to believing the best about people. For the Christian, such belief and hope are based on believing and hoping in God and in what he says in his Word about what he can do in people's lives. To put it simply: we believe in the possibilities of grace in a person's life. Left on his own, a man may look hopeless to us, but when God is added to the equation, our attitude changes. There is no such thing as a hopeless case — someone beyond the reach of God's transforming grace.

There are two extremes we must be careful to avoid, however. First, I am not advocating that we should be gullible and turn a blind eye to character flaws or our past dealings with a person. We must be clear and realistic about our reasons for seeing good potential in the lives of others. Paul often warns believers about the need to be wary of dangerous people (e.g., Acts 20:29–30; Gal. 1:7–8; 6:12–13; 2 Tim. 4:3–4), and Proverbs often warns about being a guarantor, giving a pledge, or putting up security for an unreliable person (Prov. 6:1–3; 11:15; 17:18; 22:26). This warning is especially pertinent for those who are naturally optimistic and trusting. Paul Rees suggests that we must "learn to distinguish between persons who are temperamentally optimistic and persons who are theologically hopeful."[1] That is a nice way of saying it. Our belief and hope for people arises from a theology of God's grace.

On the other extreme, though, are those who are cynical. It's hard to ignore the hypocrisy and deception we see today. Commitments are broken and leaders hide their involvement in the very sins they preach against. Political leaders make promises in election campaigns that are conveniently forgotten. In church and society selfish ambition masquerades as selfless service. Some people look at all of this and refuse to believe that people can change. They view every person they meet and every promise they hear with suspicion.[2]

But we need not adopt either extreme. The Bible has a realistic understanding of human nature. It clearly presents us as fallen, broken, trapped in slavery to our sin, and incapable of living holy lives apart from God's help. Yet it just as clearly presents God's grace as something *greater* than our sins and weaknesses. If we are cynical about people, we are showing that we have failed to truly believe the power of the gospel. So we look at people with bright hope, knowing that if they avail themselves of God's grace, they too can overcome their sins and weaknesses and become great people.

BARNABAS AND PAUL

Barnabas was a teacher and leader in the early church. He was well-known for being an encourager of others, and several times in the book of Acts we see him exhibiting this quality. He was one of the men sent by the Jerusalem church to examine the reports of a growing, young church in Antioch. Undoubtedly there were problems and shortcomings in this church. But Luke summarizes what Barnabas saw in Antioch: "He ... saw the grace of God [and] was glad" (Acts 11:23). Barnabas chose to focus on God's *grace*, looking for evidence that God was at work among these new believers rather than dwelling on the ways they fell short.

We see this graciousness again when Paul arrived for the first time in Jerusalem, following his conversion. Paul attempted to join the disciples, but they were afraid of him as a former persecutor of the church and saw him as a possible spy. They could not believe he was a disciple. But Barnabas took the risk and brought Paul to the inner circle of the apostles and certified to them the story of Paul's conversion (Acts 9:26–27).

Paul and Barnabas later became colleagues in ministry. But when they planned their second missionary journey together, Paul refused to accept John Mark because he had deserted them in a time of hardship on their first journey. Once again, Barnabas showed graciousness and love as he refused to give up on this young believer. Standing up for Mark appears to have been a costly decision for Barnabas, for Luke records that his partnership with Paul was (temporarily) suspended after a heated argument over the matter. In the end, Paul parted ways from Barnabas and John Mark, taking a man named Silas along instead (Acts 15:36–41).

But Barnabas's investment in this young disciple paid off, for John Mark is the same Mark who later penned the second gospel of the New Testament! The first great historian of the early church, Eusebius, tells us that Mark eventually travelled to Egypt and became the bishop of Alexandria. Alexandria later became one of the intellectual centers of Christianity, and today the nine-million strong Coptic Church in Egypt traces its origin to Mark's ministry.

I don't want to leave you with the impression that Paul failed to grasp this quality of trusting love, however. After all, he wrote the very verse we are studying! Paul eventually came to see people with the same gracious, hope-filled optimism as Barnabas. Let me mention two examples. The first is contained in the letter of Philemon. Paul writes this letter on behalf of a runaway slave named Onesimus, whom he affectionately calls "my son." He addresses his letter to Onesimus's master, Philemon. Paul asks Philemon to receive back his slave as a brother in Christ, even offering to pay whatever money Onesimus may have robbed from his master. Paul was able to see and expect the best in both Onesimus and Philemon, and he was willing to believe that the gospel could turn a thieving slave and a slave owner into brothers, united in Christ. God viewed this event so significant that he included the book of Philemon in the Bible!

A second example of Paul's grace-filled love toward people is seen in his words toward his protégé, Timothy, whom Paul repeatedly refers to as his own "child." In the Greek, this is not the usual word for "son" (*huios*), but a more affectionate word (*teknon*), usually translated in the ESV as "child." Timothy was a young man with a somewhat timid nature, who often needed to be exhorted and encouraged to stand strong. In 1 Timothy 1:18, we learn the motivation behind his exhortations to Timothy: "This charge I entrust to you, Timothy, my child, *in accordance with the prophecies previously made about you*, that by them you may wage the good warfare" (emphasis added). Apparently, prophecies had been made about Timothy that became the basis for Paul's ambitions for this young man. Paul is here entrusting Timothy with a "charge." This strong word conveys a sense of urgency and is used in military settings. But along with these strong words he reminds Timothy of his potential under God as indicated by the prophecies about him. Achieving this potential had become Paul's ambition. In the same way we must have ambitions for those we disciple and lead, believing in what God can do through them.

BELIEF AND HOPE AT WORK

I trust these examples help you to grasp how gracious, hope-filled optimism in the God-given potential of others is an expression of love. But what does this look like in day-to-day life? How does a trusting belief in God's power and a hopeful vision for the future lead us to love others in a practical way?

One example that immediately comes to mind is the gracious love of a forgiving wife. Consider a husband who has sinned against his wife and has had an affair. He confesses his sin to her and is truly repentant for what has happened. He humbly submits himself to the discipline of his church and is stripped of his roles and responsibilities. He genuinely wants to restore his relationship with his wife, but his wife is deeply hurt by his unfaithfulness. At first, she tries to believe the best, that he is sincerely repentant of his sins, and she fights against the temptation to be suspicious. She accepts him back and opens the door to restoring his morally shamed life.

But it is difficult to rebuild their broken trust. Rebuilding trust takes time and must be tested by experience. What if, after a lengthy process of repentance, the wife continues to remain suspicious of her husband's every move? What if, after several years, she continues to doubt his explanations when he is home late from work? What if she is constantly bringing up the past, reminding him of his unfaithfulness at every opportunity? It is difficult to restore love in that relationship. In fact, her unwillingness to graciously love and forgive her husband will likely make their home so unpleasant for her husband that he will be tempted to spend time away from her, looking for emotional satisfaction outside his marriage. This will leave him vulnerable to another affair. Obviously, unhappiness at home is never an excuse to sin. My point is simply that the wife, in her unwillingness to extend grace, is failing to sow the seeds that must develop and mature into gracious love. She is actively undermining any attempts to restore her marriage.

The word "hope" in 1 Corinthians 13:7 speaks of a bigger challenge than "belief." Hope looks beyond failure and defeat and hopeless situations to what God can do in a person. I have occasionally counseled a couple against marrying because I felt they were not well suited for each other. Sometimes the couple disregards my advice and proceeds with the marriage. Even though I may have had reservations, once they are married, I make it clear to them that remaining happily married is now God's will for them. I encourage them that God is committed to their marriage. If they have problems, I do all I can to help them. The fact that they ignored my advice is not important now. What they need is help to come out of a difficult situation, and we will give all the help we can give, believing that God is committed to the welfare of the marriage. I am thankful that some couples have proved me wrong and gone on to have happy marriages.

The example of Raja Wijekoon shows us that believing and hoping in people can result in a lot of disappointment. But there is excitement in a life lived for others. Along the road of service to others God has a way of intervening in thrilling ways that bring a spark to our life. There is a price to pay, but while so many people are complaining of boredom, we can happily say that there is no boredom in the life of love: many problems, but no boredom!

OUR HOPE GIVES HOPE TO PEOPLE

How often people get hurt by comments and attitudes of others that suggest they are hopeless people! Everyone has weaknesses, but the weaknesses of some are more conspicuous than those of others. Such people tend to be rejected as hopeless. But some of them may become great leaders, and along the way there is usually a leader or two who believed in them and gave them opportunities to serve and grow.

I consider Dr. Colton Wickremaratne to be one of the greatest leaders in the contemporary Sri Lankan church. He led the Assemblies of God in Sri Lanka from the time it was a small denomination until it became the largest Protestant denomination in our country. I once heard Dr. Colton say in a sermon that he was one of three young men in his graduating class at the Assembly of God Bible College. The other two were given ministry assignments, but not the young Colton Wickremaratne. The principal of the college, who was the head of the denomination at the time, believed that Colton had a big mouth and was not suited for ministry.

When Colton finally received an assignment, the tone with which it was given made it look like a punishment. He was to do little things like running errands for the leaders of a church and was given no tasks that we traditionally associate with pastoral ministry. Thankfully, the missionary pastor of the church to which he was sent saw something else in this young man, and he extended gracious love to him, hoping and believing that God would someday use Colton in powerful ways. He encouraged Colton and gave him opportunities to minister. Finally, believing that an indigenous leader should pastor the church, not a missionary, he gave Colton his job. From these humble beginnings, God used Dr. Colton to spread the gospel throughout Sri Lanka and bring effective leadership to God's church in our nation.

Many great leaders were at one time a nuisance to others. They had a lot of zeal but little wisdom, so they made glaring mistakes, which brought shame to their leaders. Often they tried to do too much and went ahead of others in the team. Many people were turned off by their behavior, but one or two leaders saw a heart for God behind the awkward behavior. These people encouraged and guided them without rejecting them because of their weaknesses. These young men did become more mature and became great leaders.

Henry Drummond says, "The people who influence you are the people who believe in you. In an atmosphere of suspicion men shrivel up, but in a trusting atmosphere they expand, and find encouragement and educative fellowship."[3] In our Youth for Christ ministry we have often found young people who have been marginalized and hurt by the hostile and competitive society in which we live. It is refreshing for them to find someone who believes in them, someone who genuinely believes they can be used by God for good.

I have worked most of my life with the poor, and I believe that one of the greatest gifts we can give them is to believe that God has a future for them. People who are repeatedly told that they are not significant eventually come to believe it. Their environment and the people around them tell them directly or by implication that they are inferior and destined for failure. Some of the people I work with grow so discouraged over this that they give up trying to change. Others overcome their sense of inferiority by resorting to alcohol or drugs, finding a temporary emotional boost that helps them forget their sense of inferiority. Others resort to crime and destructive behavior in order to force the world to take notice of them. A few seek to compensate by an ambition to succeed in life. While this is the best of the above reactions to rejection by society, if they maintain their anger over rejection as they climb in society, they can do great harm. Angry leaders are dangerous to the health of church and society.

We can reverse the trend of people being hurt through rejection with attitudes and actions that communicate hope. Adam Clarke (1762? – 1832) was one of the great scholars of the early Methodist movement. He was a slow learner at school. One day, a distinguished visitor paid a visit to the school, and the teacher singled out Adam Clarke with the words: "This is the stupidest boy in the school." Before leaving the school, the visitor came up to Clarke and quietly said to him, "Never mind, my boy, you may be a great scholar some day. Don't be discouraged but try hard, and keep on trying."[4] Clarke did, in fact, become a great scholar and was fluent in several languages. The great British preacher Charles Spurgeon once referred to him as "the prince of commentators." In fact, Clarke's large eight-volume commentary is still in print over two hundred years after it was written and continues to be helpful to students of the Bible.

Never underestimate what God can do in the life of a hopeless man or woman. Truthfully, we are all hopeless apart from God's grace! That is why we must offer radical love to people by letting them know that we have hope for their lives. Anyone can change through the power of the gospel.

BREAKING PATTERNS

I need to give two concluding thoughts before ending this chapter. First, we must develop "a culture of believability." When some people speak, it is impossible to trust them fully. We are always wondering, "What is really behind this statement?" A leader wants to launch a project that has five stages. But he goes to his board for permission to do it after he has already completed two stages of the project. The board realizes that it is too late to reject this proposal, so it is forced to approve it. The leader completes his project, but he loses his credibility. The members of the board come to the sad realization that they have been manipulated and that this leader is not a person of integrity.

In such cases, it is impossible to nurture a culture of believability. It is dangerous to believe such leaders because we really don't know the hidden agenda behind what they say. James insists that it is not necessary for Christians to swear. Why not? James says, "Let your 'yes' be yes and your 'no' be no" (Jas. 5:12). In other words, what they say can be trusted. Leaders like this help nurture an environment where integrity is a nonnegotiable norm. They show, through their speech and actions, that a lack of integrity is not tolerated. It is amazing how movements gradually change under that type of leadership. Those who are dishonest either change or leave as they become uncomfortable with this strong emphasis on truthfulness.

Second, those who believe and hope in people are sure to get hurt. People you have trusted will disappoint you. But remember, Jesus had a Judas. Over twenty years ago, I was in a state of shock after finding out that one of our staff had done something dishonest. I kept telling myself, "How could this have happened in Youth for Christ?" Then I read for my devotions that Judas "having charge of the moneybag ... used to help himself to what was put into it" (John 12:6). It was a comfort to me to know that even Jesus had such people. Thankfully that staff worker was restored after a time under discipline and has remained a faithful Christian ever since.

Though some will fail us and even betray the trust we placed in them, others will prove to be faithful. Perhaps they are the people whom we least expect who will make it. Some will return to a faithful Christian life much later. In our ministry we have found that several of the youth who left our fellowship as a result of backsliding return to Christ many years later and become active in their churches. When I meet them, they mention how grateful they are to Youth for Christ for the investment we made in their lives. In a different context Paul said, "And let us not grow weary of doing good, for in due season we will reap, if we do not give up" (Gal. 6:9). Let us not grow weary of believing and hoping in people.

, , ,

One of the biggest theological battles I have had in my life has been whether it is truly possible to believe that people can be transformed by grace. I have often wondered whether I am a naïve fool for believing that God can make some people into vibrant, stable, and holy Christians. But I simply cannot give into the cynicism of our age; I cannot give up hope. Why? Because the Bible tells me that there is nothing too hard for God. His grace is greater than all our sins and weaknesses. Don't let the environment in which you live ruin your hope. God is too great, too loving, and too gracious for us to let our attitude be controlled by cynicism. Keep clinging to belief in the possibilities of grace; never give up the knowledge that faith in our powerful God will transform your prayer life and drive you to be an active agent of hope in this cynical world.

CHAPTER 19

IT'S WORTH IT!

1 CORINTHIANS 13:8 – 13

MANY PEOPLE TODAY see the life of holiness as a boring and dreary commitment to duty. They wonder if it's really worth the price they pay. I know a lady who became a Christian early in her marriage. Along with her husband, she had lived a wild life before being saved by Christ. Her husband agreed to go to church with his wife, but he refused to be as committed to Christ as his wife. "I must have my fun," he said. He refused to give financially to the church, saying that he just could not afford it. Then, after many years of living a half-hearted Christianity, he decided to commit himself fully to Christ. Afterward, he admitted that half-hearted living was really not all that fun. He experienced how living *fully* for Christ is the only way to true fulfillment and lasting joy.

Paul climaxes his discussion on love by showing that the way of love is truly worthwhile. As we saw earlier, Paul began this chapter by contrasting the value of several spiritual gifts with the value of love (1 Cor. 13:1 – 3). Now, he ends by doing something similar (13:8 – 13). Earlier, Paul said that exercising gifts without love is useless. Now, as he closes, he helps us to see that not only does a lack of love render something useless, but it will not last the test of eternity. Only what is done in love will last.

PERMANENT AND TRANSITORY VALUES

Paul begins this final section of the chapter saying, "Love never ends" (1 Cor. 13:8), and he concludes it saying that only "faith, hope, and love abide" (13:13). Sandwiched between verses 8 and 13 is a section that looks at the transitory nature of some of the gifts that were so valued in Corinth. Verse 8b makes a general statement: "As for prophecies, they will pass away; as for tongues, they will cease; as for knowledge, it will pass away." There has been some debate in the church about when this passing away will take place. The context suggests that it will take place when Christ comes back — that is, at the end of history as we know it.

In verses 9 and 10 Paul applies this to two gifts in particular: knowledge and prophecy. "For we know in part and we prophesy in part, but when the perfect comes, the partial will pass away." Paul uses two illustrations to help us understand. The first is the image of a child growing to maturity: "When I was a child, I spoke like a child, I thought like a child, I reasoned like a child. When I became a man, I gave up childish ways" (13:11).

Then, Paul borrows the image of a mirror. In those days, mirrors were made of metal and they did not give as clear of an image as the glass mirrors of today. Paul tells us that now we see ourselves poorly reflected, dimly as in a mirror. But a time will come when we will see and know everything clearly. "For now we see in a mirror dimly, but then face to face. Now I know in part; then I shall know fully, even as I have been fully known" (13:12). However gifted we may be in this age, we still have limitations. Even a person with the gift of knowledge or the gift of prophecy does not know the day on which the Lord will return. When we enter the new age where we will all be with Christ face-to-face, there will no longer be a need for the gifts of tongues, prophecy, and knowledge.

As wonderful and amazing as these gifts are, they won't last forever. Yet there are some things that last. Paul mentions *three* things that abide forever: "So now faith, hope, and love abide, these three" (13:13a). Why does faith last? Because faith is an abiding trust in the word of another, and we will always, even in heaven, relate to God by trusting him for everything we have. The same is true with hope. In heaven, there will no longer be sorrow or pain. So why will we need to hope, if there is no fear that God will fail to meet our needs and keep his promises? Hope is the future-oriented aspect of our faith. Heaven will not be a static, unchanging reality. Though we do not fully understand how this will happen, we know that we will continue to actively seek God and look to him to provide for us—both in the present and in the future. We will continue to enjoy the thrill of childlike trust in the God who loves us like a father.

But as wonderful as faith and hope are, love will be the hallmark of life in the age to come. My pastor in my teenage years, the Rev. George Good, used to say that heaven is the place where human love is perfected. The love of God, expressed in the love we have for one another and the love we have for him, will be the defining mark of the heavenly community.

THE GREATEST IS LOVE

After mentioning faith, hope, and love, Paul concludes, "the greatest of these is love." Paul does not tell us *why* love is the greatest. But I think it is worth trying to speculate by using some facts that we know for sure to be true about love. First, it is no doubt true that people with faith and hope but without love are not pleasant to be around and are a bad advertisement for Christianity. We may be impressed by their trust in God and obedience based on it, but they miss the most important aspect of obedience: love for God and people. Believing that God has called them to something signifi-cant, they will bulldoze their way to fulfill their tasks. But they invariably leave behind a trail of hurt and annoyed people.

Second, loving others is the best way to represent the God who *is* love. John says, "God is love, and whoever abides in love abides in God, and God abides in him" (1 John 4:16). The surest mark of a true Christian is that he or she is a loving person. Jesus said, "Whoever keeps his word, in him truly the love of God is perfected. By this we may know that we are in him" (2:5). John says that it is love for others that attests to our own salvation: "We know that we have passed out of death into life, because we *love* the brothers. Whoever does not *love* abides in death" (1 John 3:14, emphasis mine). Love is what will ultimately show the world that Chris-tianity is true. Jesus said, "By this all people will know that you are my disciples, if you have love for one another" (John 13:35).

Rodney ("Gypsy") Smith (1860–1947) was a unique British evangelist and singer who had a long and fruitful ministry. Born in a gypsy tent, Smith never attended school. For a time he served with the Wesleyan mission in Manchester, England, and one of the women in that minis-try frequently requested prayers for the conversion of her husband, John. Sadly, she also had a terrible temper. Sometimes when her husband would be close to surrendering to the claims of Christ, she would upset him by having a temper tantrum. Her husband, confused by the disconnect between the message she was sharing and her behavior, would say, "Well, Mary, if that is religion I don't want it." She would later apologize and ask his forgiveness, but he made a habit of using her temper as his reason for not following Christ.

One day, Smith talked to the woman frankly and told her that she must learn to overcome her temper. He assured her that Christ would give her the grace to enable her to curb her habit. Believing in God, she made a commitment to start a new chapter in her life. It happened to be the time for spring cleaning. The woman had just put in new carpet and a new ceiling lamp, which she had hung up in the hallway. Her husband, John, came home carrying something on his shoulder, and did not know there was a new lamp. As he turned the corner, he hit the lamp and it all came crashing down to the ground in scattered pieces.

John braced for his wife's usual response, a torrent of angry words and berating comments. But instead of the typical response, John was surprised to hear nothing. Instead, his wife looked down over the stairs at him and simply said, "Never mind, husband! It is all right; we can get another lamp." Confused and surprised, John looked up at her.

"Mary, what's the matter?"

She calmly replied, "O, my dear, I have trusted Jesus to cure me of my temper."

John, still amazed at his wife's unexpected response, said, "Well, if he has cured you, come right down and pray for me, for that's what I want. If there is enough in religion to cure your temper, I want the same religion." After years of prayers, John was converted that very day.[1]

LOVE BRINGS JOYOUS BRIGHTNESS

The third reason I present for love being the greatest is that love brings joyous brightness to life. Surprisingly, there is much in the Bible that speaks of a direct link between love and joy. Love is typically presented as the defining feature of a Christian's *lifestyle*. Joy is presented as a basic *result* of being a Christian. Those who live in love experience joy—it immediately follows love in the list of the fruit of the Spirit in a person's life (Gal. 5:22). Joy, like love, comes from God and not from within a person.

Love leads to the completion or fulfillment of our joy. Paul writes that when Christians are "of the same mind, having the same *love*, being in full accord and of one mind," it completes his joy (Phil. 2:2, emphasis added). David says, "Behold, how good and pleasant it is when brothers dwell in unity!" (Ps. 133:1). Where real love is practiced, joy is the result. People are naturally happy about the love they experience and share together.

My former colleague and good friend Adrian de Visser told me about an incident that took place when he went to the home of Dr. Joel Hunter, Senior Pastor of the Northland Church in Orlando. Dr. Hunter's wife was bringing the main dish to the dining table when she tripped and fell. The dish crashed to the ground and its contents were splattered in all directions on the floor. Adrian wondered how Dr. Hunter would react. He ran to her and asked, "Are you hurt, honey?" When he found out that she was not, he looked at Adrian and said, "Adrian, there are plenty of places where we could go and eat anything we want, but I'm so glad that Becky is not hurt." Here is love practiced as Paul has been describing in 1 Corinthians 13. I think that once Becky got over the shock of the accident, as she reflected on her husband's reaction, it would have given her a sense of joy over his love for her. When people keep experiencing this kind of love, they are going to be happy people.

We must remember that the joy of love is often experienced, most evidently, in the context of sacrificially serving one another, just as Christ has served us. Imagine a wife who wakes up with a splitting headache. Her husband makes her breakfast and brings it to her bed before going to work. When he comes home from work, she is still struggling with a headache. He had been hoping to watch a football game on TV, but instead he cooks her dinner, insisting that she rest. Even in the midst of her pain, there is joy because she knows that her husband has demonstrated his love to her by sacrificially serving her.

The next day when her husband comes from work, she welcomes him with open arms, clearly displaying her satisfaction over seeing him. He relishes this display of love. So the next day he wants to come home as soon as possible to be with his wife. He is so different from his colleague who sometimes takes on extra work so that he can delay going home to his nagging wife. Some days he goes to the bar and gets drunk to avoid feeling the sting of his wife's rebukes. But the next day he gets up with a hangover and the sure prospects of facing his wife's wrath, which makes him want to get drunk again!

Coming back to the story of our happy home, imagine that one day the elder son comes home while his mother is busy preparing dinner and is stressed out with all that has to be done. As he opens the door, he shouts, "Mummy." Her first instinct is to shout, "What?" in a harsh tone. But decisive love wins through. She decides to still the voice of annoyance and respond kindly saying, "What is it, son?" He excitedly announces that he has been selected to the school basketball team. She reacts to this news with glee and shouts for the other children to come. With them she prays and thanks God for blessing her son. When his father comes home, the son rushes up to his dad and gives him the good news. The father says, "I know, son, your mother already called me and gave me the good news." The son is thrilled with the response of his family.

Where do you think this son will go when he has a problem in school or when he struggles with the uncertainties of his relationships with members of the opposite sex? To his mother! He knows she will listen, try to understand him, and give him kind advice. In order to get the attention of a listening ear, he does not need to go to his friends who do not follow Christian principles and would probably give him bad advice. He knows he has a listening ear at home.

Can you see the rewards when decisive Christian love is practiced in the home? In each of these episodes, a decision had to be made to respond lovingly to a situation for which the natural reaction would have been one of annoyance. But when we keep responding to challenging situations at home with decisive love, an atmosphere of joy will pervade the home.

WHEN LOVE IS NOT RECIPROCATED

But what if you don't have a spouse who loves you in the way we have described? What if your children remain angry and rebellious despite all your efforts to be kind and considerate to them? What if you seek to offer love to someone, but it is not reciprocated? This can be hard for a loving Christian to endure. It is hard to pour out love, yet not receive a loving response in return. But we can go to God when we are hurt in this way. He listens to us and understands our pain, and he will surely comfort us. We may express our pain through lament, as we saw in chapter 4, and God will listen to us sympathetically.

Recall what happened to Stephen when he was dying. He was facing bitter anger and wickedness against him, but his words and actions showed that he was close to Christ. He had a vision of Christ, standing like a witness speaking on behalf of him in the divine tribunal at a time the earthly tribunal had condemned him to die. He said the things Christ said when he was dying, and he was in communion with him to the end. Paul spoke of the fellowship of sharing in Christ's sufferings (Phil. 3:10) when referring to the depth of union with Christ that can be experienced only as we suffer as he did. Stephen had entered into this. While he faced rejection on earth, he was experiencing a new depth of intimacy with and acceptance by God. That would have made all the pain worthwhile.

So even in situations where love is not reciprocated, it is worthwhile loving because the suffering of rejection deepens our love relationship with Christ. Our relationship with Christ is the most beautiful thing in our lives. Therefore deep down, we will experience the deepest joy of being close to Christ.

A lady was being scolded in abusive language by her husband. As she listened to him berate her, she suddenly recalled that people had said similar things to Jesus when he was on earth. What she was going through was similar to the suffering of Christ, and this knowledge brought her great comfort. It helped her to forgive her husband and even to lovingly care for him later as he was dying. She ended her days on earth as a widow filled with the love and joy of Christ. Though she had a difficult life, she knew that Jesus had been good to her. She had a loving Savior, and this gave her comfort. Her life was most influenced by the love of God, not by the unkindness others had shown her.

, , ,

There is great value in a life devoted to love. It is costly. Sometimes it means that we will be inconvenienced. Often we must act against our natural instincts and make decisions to follow what we know to be the loving path. But it is worth it! As Paul says, Love is the "more excellent way" (1 Cor. 12:31). And why?

- Humans are made in the image of the God who is love, and when they live lives of love, they become truly human.
- Since love is intimately connected to the joy of the Lord, those who exercise love become joyous people.
- When exercised biblically, love brings healing to the wounds inflicted on us by uncaring people.
- When we live lives of love, we express the highest value in Christianity, which supersedes the value of great ability and voluminous achievements.
- In a unique way our love witnesses to the beauty of the saving gospel of Jesus Christ before a watching world.
- God's provision of strength to love enables us to live according to the high principles of Christian love, so that we can experience the *shalom* of a life where action does not contradict belief.

- The rewards of love are eternal and well worth the price paid for it on earth.
- Love is going to be our preoccupation for eternity. Our present lives are but a training ground for the opportunity to fully experience and apply love.

A wise person, therefore, would do well to follow Paul's advice: "Make love your aim" (1 Cor. 14:1 RSV).

NOTES

INTRODUCTION: FOLLOWING THE WAY OF LOVE

1. J. B. Phillips, *The New Testament in Modern English* (rev. ed.; New York: Macmillan, 1972), 318.

2. C. E. B. Cranfield, *The Epistle to the Romans* (International Critical Commentary; Edinburgh: T&T Clark, 1975), 1:263.

3. Taken from Corrie ten Boom, *Clippings from My Notebook* (Nashville, TN: Nelson, 1982), 92–94.

4. Author not given, *Fourth Gospel* (3rd ed.; Bangalore, India: The Association for Theological Education by Extension, 2010), 64.

5. Leon Morris, *1 Corinthians: An Introduction and Commentary* (Tyndale New Testament Commentaries; Downers Grove, IL: InterVarsity Press, 1985). Electronic version, Logos Bible Software.

6. Taken from Robertson McQuilkin, "Living by Vows" (Columbia, SC: Columbia International University), a reprint of an article that originally appeared in *Christianity Today* in 1990.

CHAPTER 1: GREATER THAN SPECTACULAR GIFTS

1. Roy E. Ciampa and Brian S. Rosner, *The First Letter to the Corinthians* (Pillar New Testament Commentary; Grand Rapids: Eerdmans, 2010). Electronic version, Logos Bible Software.

2. See David Gill, "1 Corinthians," in *Zondervan Illustrated Bible Background Commentary* (ed. Clinton E. Arnold; Grand Rapids: Zondervan, 2002), 3:167. Electronic version, Pradis 6.0.

3. The story is related in Dennis F. Kinlaw, *The Mind of Christ* (Nappance, IN: Evangel, 1998), 72–73; and recorded in my book *The Call to Joy and Pain* (Wheaton, IL: Crossway, 2007), 71–72.

4. Taken from an article by Robert Docter in the Salvation Army

e-magazine *New Frontier* (www.newfrontierpublications.org/nf/
on-the-corner-the-springs-of-sacred-service/).

5. Leslie T. Lyall, *A Passion for the Impossible* (London: Hodder &
Stoughton, 1965).

CHAPTER 2: GREATER THAN RADICAL COMMITMENT

1. Henry Drummond, *The Greatest Thing in the World* (Springdale, PA:
Whitaker House, 1981), 18.

2. Gerald L. Sittser, *Water from a Deep Well: Christian Spirituality from
Early Martyrs to Modern Missionaries* (Downers Grove, IL: InterVarsity Press, 2007), 319, n. 38.

3. Related by Grace Dube in Jan Pit, compiler, *Bound to be Free: With the
Suffering Church* (Tonbridge, UK: Sovereign World, 1995), 200–202.

CHAPTER 3: PATIENCE WITH WEAKNESSES

1. See the book by Gary Chapman, *Love Is a Verb: Stories of What Happens When Love Comes Alive* (Minneapolis: Bethany, 2010).

2. David E. Garland, *1 Corinthians* (Baker Exegetical Commentary on
the New Testament; Grand Rapids: Baker Academic, 2003), 616.

3. *Makrothymeō* and the corresponding noun can also be used in rela-
tion to enduring trials. However, we will look at the issue of enduring trials in our discussion of endurance (*hypomenō*) in verse 7.

4. Robertson's exact words are: "The Holy Spirit lays hold of our weaknesses along with (*sun*) us and carries his part of the burden facing
us (*anti*) as if two men were carrying a log at each end." Cited in
R. Kent Hughes, *Romans: Righteousness from Heaven* (Wheaton, IL:
Crossway, 1991), 163.

5. William D. Mounce, gen ed., *Mounce's Expository Dictionary of Old
and New Testament Words* (Grand Rapids: Zondervan, 2006), 139.

CHAPTER 4: PATIENCE WITH SIN

1. In addition to the two passages mentioned in the previous paragraph,
the other passages are: Romans 2:4; 9:22; 1 Peter 3:20; 2 Peter 3:15.

2. Corrie ten Boom, *Clippings*, 83.

3. Corrie ten Boom with John and Elizabeth Sherrill, *The Hiding Place*
(Minneapolis: World Wide Pictures, n.d. original edition, 1971), 204.

4. Ibid., 208.

5. This observation was made by the Rev. Ebenezer Joseph, past president of the Methodist Church of Sri Lanka, at a conference, "Freed to Forgive," held in Colombo, Sri Lanka, on January 10, 2012.
6. R. T. Kendall, *Total Forgiveness: Achieving God's Greatest Challenge* (London: Hodder and Stoughton, 2001), 175.
7. Lewis Smedes, *Forgive and Forget: Healing the Hurt We Don't Deserve* (San Francisco: Harper & Row, 1984), 133.
8. Wess Stafford, "A Candle in the Darkness," *Christianity Today* (May 2010), 23–26.
9. Wess Stafford, response in *Christianity Today* (July 2010), 43.

CHAPTER 5: PATIENCE ENCOUNTERING JUSTICE

1. Edward John Carnell, *Christian Commitment* (New York: Macmillan, 1957), 94–95; quoted in John Piper, *Future Grace* (Sisters OR: Multnomah, 1995), 265. Carnell adds that though we do not have the right to complete the moral cycle and take matters of justice into our own hands, "we sense no spiritual inhibition against crying out against injustice."
2. John Wesley, *The Works of John Wesley: Journals,* June 11, 1778 (Albany, OR: Ages Software). Electronic edition, Logos Bible Software.
3. Mrs. Arthur Parker, *Sadhu Sundar Singh: Called of God* (Madras: Christian Literature Society, 1918), 25–26.
4. J. R. Edwards, *Romans* (New International Biblical Commentary; Peabody, MA: Hendrickson, 1992), 299; in Logos Bible Software.

CHAPTER 6: CONCERN IN ACTION

1. Paul Sangster, *Dr. Sangster* (London: Epworth, 1962), 54; cited in Warren W. Wiersbe and Lloyd M. Perry, *Wycliffe Handbook of Preaching and Preachers* (Chicago: Moody Press, 1984), 216–17.
2. Garland, *1 Corinthians,* 617.
3. Murray J. Harris, *Slave of Christ: A New Testament Metaphor for Total Devotion to Christ* (Leicester, UK, and Downers Grove, IL: InterVarsity Press, 1999).
4. St. John Chrysostom, *The Love Chapter: The Meaning of First Corinthians 13,* Contemporary English edition (Brewster, MA: Paraclete, 2010), xiii. This book is extracted from his larger homilies on the New Testament.

5. Ibid., 33.

6. Sandra Wilson, *Hurt People Hurt People: Hope and Healing for Yourself and Your Relationships* (Grand Rapids: Discovery House, 2001).

7. A. T. Robertson, *Epochs in the Life of the Apostle John* (Grand Rapids: Baker, 1974 reprint), 106.

8. Taken almost verbatim from ibid., 106.

CHAPTER 7: IS IT WORTH SHOWING KINDNESS?

1. Murray J. Harris, *The Second Epistle to the Corinthians* (The New International Greek Testament Commentary; Grand Rapids: Eerdmans, 2005), 418.

2. Ibid., 419.

3. Matt. 22:39; Mark 12:31, 33; Luke 10:27; Rom 13:9; Gal. 5:14; James 2:8 (see also Matt. 5:43; Rom. 13:10).

4. Francis Schaeffer, *The Church at the End of the Twentieth Century* (London: Hodder & Stoughton, 1970), 189.

5. Bryan A. Follis, *Truth with Love: The Apologetics of Francis Schaeffer* (Wheaton, IL: Crossway, 2006).

6. Rodney Stark, *The Rise of Christianity: How the Obscure, Marginal Jesus Movement Became the Dominant Religious Force in the Western World in a Few Centuries* (San Francisco: HarperSanFrancisco, 1997), 73–94.

7. Cited by Becky Pippert at the Urbana Missionary Conference in 1987.

8. Paul Lee Tan, *Encyclopedia of 7700 Illustrations: Signs of the Times* (Garland, TX: Bible Communications, Inc., 1996). #4365. Electronic version, Logos Bible Software.

CHAPTER 8: ENVY VERSUS SHOWING HONOR

1. Bruce M. Metzger, *Lexical Aids for Students of New Testament Greek* (Princeton: Theological Book Agency, 1970), 37.

2. J. P. Louw and E. A. Nida, *Greek-English Lexicon of the New Testament: Based on Semantic Domains* (New York: United Bible Societies, 1996), 297, 759. Electronic edition, Logos Bible Software.

3. D. A. Carson, *Showing the Spirit: A Theological Exposition of 1 Corinthians 12–14* (Grand Rapids: Baker, 1987), 62.

4. Raymond McHenry, *McHenry's Quips, Quotes, & Other Notes* (Peabody, MA: Hendrickson, 1999). From the electronic edition by HeavenWord Inc.

5. Taken from Dennis F. Kinlaw, *Preaching in the Spirit* (Grand Rapids: Zondervan, 1985), 104.

CHAPTER 9: ACCEPTING WHO WE ARE: THE ANTIDOTE TO ENVY

1. J. I. Packer, *Knowing God* (Downers Grove, IL: InterVarsity Press, 1973), 181.
2. Ibid., 182.
3. Neil T. Anderson, *Victory over the Darkness: Realizing the Power of our Identity in Christ* (Ventura, CA: Regal, 1990). See especially pp. 45–47 and 57–59.
4. Sokreaksa S. Himm with Jan Greenough, *The Tears of My Soul* (London: Monarch Books, 2003), 76.
5. Ibid., 115–16.
6. Ibid., 117.

CHAPTER 10: SHARING WITHOUT BOASTING

1. Carson, *Showing the Spirit*, 62.
2. Gordon D. Fee, *The First Epistle to the Corinthians* (Grand Rapids: Eerdmans, 1987), 637–38.
3. Ciampa and Rosner, *First Letter to the Corinthians*, 644.
4. William Barclay, *Letters to the Corinthians* (3rd ed.; New Daily Study Bible; Louisville: Westminster John Knox, 2002), 139. From the electronic version of Logos Bible Software.
5. Cited in John R. W. Stott, *I Believe in Preaching* (London: Hodder & Stoughton, 1982; US title: *Between Two Worlds: The Challenge of Preaching* [Grand Rapids: Eerdmans, 1982]), 325.

CHAPTER 11: ARROGANCE: A SIGN OF WEAKNESS

1. M. L. Soards, *1 Corinthians* (New International Biblical Commentary; Peabody, MA: Hendrickson, 1999), 277.
2. 1 Cor. 4:6, 18, 19; 5:2; 8:1; 13:4; Col 2:18.
3. A. Morgan Derham, in *The New International Dictionary of the Christian Church* (ed. J. D. Douglas; Grand Rapids: Zondervan, 1978). Electronic edition, Pradis software, 2002–2004.
4. Barclay, *Letters to the Corinthians*, 142–43.
5. R. T. France, *Jesus the Radical* (Leicester, UK: Inter-Varsity Press, 1989), 43. France cites Origen, *Contra Celsum* 1.32.

6. Ibid., 45.
7. I. Howard Marshall, "Son of Man," in *Dictionary of Jesus and the Gospels* (ed. Joel B. Green, Scott McKnight, and I. Howard Marshall; Downers Grove, IL: InterVarsity Press, 1992), 781.

CHAPTER 12: SENSITIVITY TO OTHERS

1. Barclay, *Letters to the Corinthians*, 143.
2. Fee, *First Epistle to the Corinthians*, 638.
3. Louw and Nida, *Greek-English Lexicon*, 1:758.
4. See Roland Muller, *Honor and Shame: Unlocking the Door* (Bloomington, IN: Xlibris, 2000), 52.
5. Gill, "1 Corinthians," 3:157.
6. David Aikmen, *Great Souls: Six Who Changed a Century* (Lanham, MD: Lexington, 2003), 67.
7. See http://anchoryourlife.com/prayer/place.htm; and www.theranch.org/My-Prayer-Closet.109.0.html.
8. Peter T. O'Brien, *Colossians, Philemon* (Word Biblical Commentary; Waco, TX: Word, 1982), 242.

CHAPTER 13: VICTORY THROUGH SURRENDER

1. E. Stanley Jones, *Victory through Surrender* (Nashville: Abingdon, 1966).
2. Ibid., 121.

CHAPTER 14: ANGER: THE VICE OF THE VIRTUOUS

1. Drummond, *Greatest Thing in the World*, 30–31.
2. Leon Morris, in *New Dictionary of Theology* (ed. Sinclair B. Ferguson and J. I. Packer; Downers Grove, IL: InterVarsity Press, 2000), 732. Electronic edition, Logos Bible Software.

CHAPTER 15: LEARNING THE DISCIPLINE OF NOT RECKONING

1. Louw and Nida, *Greek-English Lexicon*, 1:345.
2. Related in Gerard Kelly, *Shepherd's Bush and King's Cross Study Guide* (Uckfield, East Sussex: Spring Harvest, 2003), 35; as reported by Tony Campolo, *Let Me Tell you a Story* (Nelson: Word, 2000).
3. See Sangster, *Dr. Sangster*, 169; cited in Wiersbe and Perry, *Wycliffe Handbook*, 216.

4. C. John Miller, *The Heart of a Servant Leader: Letters from Jack Miller* (ed. Barbara Miller Juliani; Phillipsburg, NJ: P&R, 2004), 209.

5. David Seamands, *Healing for Damaged Emotions* (Wheaton, IL: Victor, 1981), 97–98.

6. Ibid., 30–31.

CHAPTER 16: LOVE FOCUSES ON THE TRUTH, NOT ON WRONG

1. Leon Morris, *Reflections on the Gospel of John*; vol. 2, *The Bread of Life* (Grand Rapids: Baker, 1987), 377. A one-volume edition covering the entire gospel of John is now available—pure gold!

2. David Hocking, *Chapter 13: Where Love Begins* (Eugene, OR: Harvest House, 1992), 157.

3. Cited in R. H. Mounce, "Gospel," *Evangelical Dictionary of Theology* (ed. Walter A. Elwell; Grand Rapids: Baker, 1984), 472 (I have modernized Tyndale's archaic English).

4. Quoted in Ruth Connell, compiler, *More Precious than Gold: Psalm 19* (Herts, UK: Lion, 1985), 32.

5. C. S. Lewis, *The Four Loves* (London: Geoffrey Bles, 1960), 92.

CHAPTER 17: LOVE'S PERSEVERANCE

1. Barclay, *Letters to the Corinthians*, 138.

2. Leon Morris, *The Epistle to the Romans* (Pillar New Testament Commentary; Grand Rapids: Eerdmans, 1988), 325. Electronic version, Logos Bible Software.

3. Barclay, *Letters to the Corinthians*, 146.

4. Ciampa and Rosner, *First Letter to the Corinthians*, 649.

5. D. L. Moody, "Courage and Enthusiasm," in *Classic Sermons on Christian Service* (compiled by Warren Wiersbe; Grand Rapids: Kregel, 1990), 69–70.

CHAPTER 18: GRACE-FILLED: NEITHER GULLIBLE NOR CYNICAL

1. Paul S. Rees, *Triumphant in Trouble: Studies in 1 Peter* (Westwood, NJ: Revell, 1962), 26.

2. This contrast between gullible and cynical persons comes from Lewis Smedes, *Love within Limits: Realizing Selfless Love in a Selfish*

World (Grand Rapids: Eerdmans, 1978), 104. He writes, "Somewhere between the gullible person and the cynic is the wise critic."

3. Drummond, *Greatest Thing in the World,* 33–36.

4. Adapted from Barclay, *Letters to the Corinthians,* 146.

CHAPTER 19: IT'S WORTH IT!

1. Taken from "Gypsy" Smith, "How a Husband Was Converted," appearing in Singapore: *The Methodist Message* (March 2011), 4.